THE HAPPY BLACK DAUGHTER

5 Success Principles My Father Taught Me

Allison Braham

JWG
PUBLISHING HOUSE
PUBLISHING

THE HAPPY BLACK DAUGHTER

Praises for the Happy Black Daughter

"Allison's book is an important one. Touching and poignant, she paints a vivid picture of her own defining relationship with her father, all the while reinforcing the idea that the context of the black family is not always one of abandonment and dysfunction. A welcome new voice who in sharing her own story, challenges the stereotypes that too often perpetuate societal belief systems."

Jessica Huie MBE,
Author of,
Purpose: Find Your Truth and Embrace Your Calling

"This book takes the reader on an adventure of love, loss, laughter and life; captured beautifully through the special connection of a father and his daughter. Allison Braham brilliantly reminds us of the power in shaping life's challenging experiences, in a way that uses us to become better versions of ourselves. Her authentic and descriptive storytelling about the relationship with her father gives the readers a window into hard won principles of success. This book is inspiring, real and contains a message of hope that the world needs to hear."

Devon Bandison
Success Coach
Bestselling Author: "Fatherhood is Leadership":
Your Playbook for Success,
Self-Leadership and a Richer Life"

"The Happy Black Daughter, 5 Success Principles My Father Taught Me, is a brilliant read. It is quite captivating and well-illustrated, I believe the readers are in for a great treat. Allison has changed the narrative about black fathers and have intrinsically laid the path for conversations rarely had. Her creativity and storytelling are unmatched as she relays the benefits of the presence of fathers in the home and in their daughters' lives. She paints a vivid picture of her father 'the joker' that the reader can't help but to love a man they've never met. Having love and then to lose it is difficult, but the special connection she shared with her dad was an emotional reminder of the love God has for us, His children. Inspiring, didactic and brilliant is how I would describe the Happy Black Daughter.

Joan W.G,
CEO & Global Multiple Streams
Revenue Business Coach,
Bestselling Author: "From Brokenness to Victory" and
"You are Different for A Reason"

DEDICATION

This book is dedicated to my beloved father
who taught me discipline and love.

&

To all the great fathers who are doing
the best they can for their children.

Thank you.

CONTENTS

Acknowledgement

Tupac Shakur once said, "I will spark the brain that will change the world." There were so many people along my writing journey who sparked my brain and inspired me to write this book in a way that would be authentic and impactful. For their work on this book: Joan Wright Good, my publisher and her team, thank you for your guidance and expertise. Devon Bandison, my coach and friend. Thank you for your leadership, your listening ear, and your belief in me. To my Game Changer Mastermind friends, thank you. Ayo Sekai, thank you for your friendship and your perpetual support. Jason and Jodi Womack, one of my spark changers. Our encounter led me to find the strength and courage to take the writing of this book seriously. Jessica Huie, your graciousness is appreciated dearly. Minna Salami, a pure gem whose work and amazing Ted Talk has inspired me and helped me approach this book in a more transformative way. Thank you for your kindness and encouraging words. Dr. Jennifer Mascaro, thank you for taking the time to have the conversation about fatherhood and sharing with me your work on such an important topic. To my brothers Edward, Mark, Rue-Scott, Tony thank you for your ever-loving support. Our father is proud of all of us. My mother Dorcas, you are my everything. You are the wind beneath my wings. Your strength and love are incomparable.

I love you. To all the fathers and daughters who participated in this project, Anselmo Estwick, Eric Larkin, Marc Jajoute, Cassandra Estwick, Shelbi Larkin, Patricia Walker and Bintou Bah, your stories will inspire many all over the world. Thank you. I am forever grateful.

5 SUCCESS PRINCIPLES MY FATHER TAUGHT ME

Love never gets lost, it's only kept.
-African Proverb

INTRODUCTION

The Happy Black Daughter was birthed out of the loss of my own father, whose relationship I cherished so much because of all the great lessons and values he instilled in his children. He made such an impact on me, his daughter. I believe the relationship between a father and daughter is quite different than the relationship between father and son. In this book, I wanted to highlight my father's contribution to my rearing by sharing some memorable stories he and I had. I also wanted to include other black fathers who have had meaningful relationships with their daughters just to put that hush on the stereotypical myth that Black fathers are not there for their children. There are daughters whose fathers are present. There are daughters who are not "daddyless", or "father-less". The truth is that there are a lot of black women who are fatherless, and that comes with its own circumstances and consequences.

The intention of this book is not to negate the reality that there are a lot of fathers who are not present in their children's life, but to highlight those fathers who are present and have had an influential role in their daughter's lives, such as my own father. There are women who have had quality relationships with their fathers. Because of that, they are who they are today. They can make certain decisions based on their experiences with their father. They have given each other the gift of love and appreciation.

Growing up, I often heard black men being demonized by society, the society where people spoke about black men with anger and disdain. The society where black men are called out of their names. Dark, stereotypical views about black men and black fathers only perpetuate this one-dimensional image of black men. For me, I never understood what some people, or even some news outlets were talking about when they would talk down black men or black fathers in particular, calling them dead beat fathers because I never experienced that. Those views were never a reflection of my reality with my father. Because of that, I couldn't empathize with them.

I was always proud to speak about my father and share amazing stories about him. He was always a focal figure in my life. I cannot remember a time in which he was not there for me. There are many stories of daughters who share the same sentiment. Their fathers were always available to them. They were always there.

The truth is the role of a dad is no different from the role of the mom. In recent years, black fathers have taken on a very important and active role in their children's lives. Taking them to school, helping them with their homework, reading them bedtime stories at nights before they go to bed are just a few examples. Dads are even in the kitchen cooking. Newsflash! There have always been black fathers who have been there for their children generations before, including my own father. It just seems that society tends to focus more on a one-dimensional storyline. In a 2014 Huffington Post article entitled, "5 Lies We Should Stop Telling about Black Fatherhood," the number one lie that was told was, "Black fathers aren't involved in their children's life." Statistics shows that black fathers are indeed present, and the new millennials are highlighting that young black fathers are steadily involved with their children.

While reading this book, I hope you get to understand how my father played an important role in my life, and how his Journey through life helped shaped mine. His "5 fatherhood principles" that he instilled in me has helped me want to live a more meaningful life. Those principles, as my father would often say to me, "will carry you far". As your eyes gently move side to side while reading my loving story about our relationship, I hope you will begin to realize that those said stereotypes that have been embedded into the consciousness of society is only an illusion. These are false perceptions about the black father. You will gain access to the connective bond I shared with my father and the subtle and not so subtle advice and encouragement he gave throughout my life.

You will also meet 4 other daughters who I've interviewed about their own relationship with their fathers. You will see how the impact of their relationships helped shaped their foundation. You will get to see how these amazing daughters received consistent, unconditional love from their fathers, the kind of love that is the seed of happiness given to them. That seed of love has helped them make necessary life changing decisions.

Journey along as I share a little about my father's humble beginnings and about our journey together. We have given each other the gift of love and appreciation, in which many fathers and daughters have also shared. I will share those 5 success principles my father instilled in me, which I hope will inspire and move you. I hope you enjoy reading about the impact my father has made on my life. I strongly believe that black fatherhood needs to be celebrated. Great fathers need to be acknowledged. Without them we perish. Fathers have a duty to impart a sense of love and guidance to their children.

I felt right after my father transitioned, that I had the duty to honor him and celebrate him. These wonderful daughters that you'll get to read about will be doing the same. All are from different cultural backgrounds with different points of view. I hope you see that there are amazing black fathers who are literally helping to shape the lives of their daughters by using the one vital tool there is in the world, LOVE.

.... 1 ....
THE HOPEFUL IMMIGRANT

"**L**et me go," my father said as he laid on the gurney with his eyes sunken into their sockets, looking into my eyes smiling while the pain throbs throughout his body. "Let me go," his delicate voice murmured. "I'm strong." How could I let go of a man who has always been there for me? Where do I go from here? Why doesn't he want to be saved? "Don't leave me, daddy! Don't go!"

So, there I was sitting in the living room watching my father getting almost every answer to the Jeopardy questions right. He never ceased to amaze me whenever Jeopardy came on. It was always a "Shhh, don't talk. My show is on," or "Be quiet." in that authoritative tone, which meant that he was going to be laser focused and needed to concentrate on every question. The blue screen appears, and Alex Trebek narrates the most puzzling question in the category of World History. Dad has five seconds to answer. I'm staring at him as he knitted his brows in thinking mode. The countdown begins, 1 Mississippi, 2 Mississippi, 3 Mississippi, 4 Mississippi, 5 Mississippi.... Boom! He answers. Score!

"How much was that for dad?" I asked smiling. He answered, "That was for a thousand dollars."

It was times like these I relished because I learned so much about my father. He taught me so much about life, often without even realizing it. Allow me to tell you about a man, my father who had hopes and dreams like many fathers do, not just for themselves but for their children too.

My father was born in 1936, a year that will forever change my life. He was introduced into the world at a time when a small Caribbean island was in its seven-year mark of the Great Depression. This island was trying to come out of oppression, trying to find a voice, and find its own identity. It was a time where Jamaica's culture was rooted in a distant land. England was still the 'Motherland' for most of the Caribbean. King George the VI, also the head of state of Jamaica, was in his 11th day as king. These were transformative times in Jamaica. These were the times of the transition from a Colonial era to a national Jamaican society.

My grandfather, Egbert, who named my father, Alfredo, after his best friend from Cuba was the direct beneficiary of the colonial times. The customary traditions my grandfather learned, he passed down to my father. Knife and fork must be set on the table for dinner. Elbows off the table. No scraping sound of the fork and knife against the plates. Sundays the family had to eat together with the table dressed in the option of two different types of meats, usually beef or chicken. There were times when my grandfather had helpers, or maids, in the home helping with the domestic chores as he was a man of many titles. He was a Shoemaker, a butcher, as well as a tailor. He was always working away from home, but never on a Sunday.

My father Alfredo grew up with a mixture of that old British Colonial tradition combined with the vibrant, spirited African culture of Jamaica. He commanded a prestigious etiquette which he learned from his father and the community he grew up in. He was a very quiet young man nicknamed by some of the neighborhood women as, 'The Little Gentleman.' He told me that he would not dare pass by an adult and not say, "Good morning," or "Good evening." If he did, those same adults would hurriedly pay a visit to his parents, and he would indeed get a lashing. Politeness and respect were the utmost standards. Spanish Town, Jamaica in the 1940's and 1950's where my father was born, was a very genteel, prim, and proper town. Everyone knew everyone, and it was very important for a young child to always behave and show their best self in the presence of an adult.

In school, my father enjoyed playing many sports such as cricket. He played as a wicketkeeper and as a batsman at times. He loved track and field. He was no Usain Bolt, but he ran track and field like his name was Mr. Cheetah. He never missed practice, in fact, he was passionate about being at practice. My father would show up early before practice just because he wanted the coach to see that he was serious, and he was. Almost every track and field competition, my father would come in 1st place. He prided himself on showing up early and being disciplined in his actions if he wanted to win. He grew to love the likes of the late 1940's Jamaican track stars such as Herb McKenley, George Rhoden and Arthur Wint. He admired their athletic capabilities.

After school, it was important for my father to find his way home as soon as school was dismissed. He had great enthusiasm when it came to sports, but he had a whole lot of respect for my grandfather. If he was not home as soon as school was finished, he would be in trouble. My grandfather was a tall, broad-shouldered man with long arms. If you looked closely, it was as if they were touching the ground when he walked. His father, my great-grandfather, John Richmond Vidal Braham, a white Store Keeper/ Pen Keeper who later became a lay minister in the Anglican church raised my grandfather with the same discipline and work ethic. You work hard; then you will reap the benefits. "Welcome to Jamrock, camp where the
thugs dem camp at
Two-pound ah weed inna van back
It inna your hand bag, your knapsack, it inna your backpack
The smell ah give your girlfriend contact
Some boy nuh know dis, dem only come around like tourist On the beach with a few club sodas
Bedtime stories, and pose like dem name
Chuck Norris
And don't know the real hardcore"
-Damian 'Junior Gong' Marley

Life in Jamaica, in the 40's and 50's did not offer many opportunities. It wasn't the same Jamrock that Entertainers brag about today. Most men tended to the fields, cutting sugar cane. Farm work was plentiful, and men would work on the road, building things. The women did more domestic work such as washing and ironing clothes for the upper-class families. The small island of Jamaica offered beautiful sunshine and pristine beaches, however, for a young man, my dad's options were limited. My grandfather Egbert wanted the best for his son. Daddy Egbert, as I called him, wanted my father to have a quality education and a fruitful life. England would be the country to offer that. After all Jamaica was a colony of England, and it only made sense to send your son to the best of the best. England was the dream. My father's eldest sister, Esmie, who was already residing in England in the early 50's, wrote a letter to my grandfather insisting that England was indeed the country to start a new life and that Rue (my father's nickname) would like it there. "He can get a good job and make out just fine," she wrote. Daddy Egbert couldn't have been more joyful to hear those reassuring words in that letter.

The ticket was bought, and off to Kingston harbor my father went; a sendoff to the mother country for a better life. As my father voyaged off into the sunset to this distant land, he heard so much about, he recanted to me that he felt excited, but he was nervous. He was hopeful and optimistic about this new chapter of his life, but leaving behind Daddy Braham and his mum, my dad's mother, was hard to do.

The experience on the ship wasn't so bad considering the first two days he was seasick and couldn't wait to get off.

Dad wasn't always inclined to volunteer stories about his past, but if asked about it he would divulge all that he could about his experiences. I'm so grateful for the opportunity to have asked him these questions about his past. I was able to ask him questions about anything and everything, and he would answer them. He communicated to me what he needed me to hear, and there was always a lesson to learn from it.

Once on the ship, my father remembered eating salted pork and chicken, which had no flavor. He would daydream about Daddy Braham's cooking and would long for some good red peas soup, his favorite. He couldn't wait to have a good meal once he was off, but he would have to endure the monthlong journey. There was some entertainment on the ship; there would be singing and a little dancing here and there, some of which he joined in.

There were many Jamaican families migrating to England from Jamaica during the late 40's and 50's with hopes and big dreams. My father was going to be a part of that. They were aspiring, most of them young black Caribbean men traveling to the "motherland" for a better life. As a young nineteen-year-old man in 1955, relocating to another country created anxiety and excitement for dad. However, the thought of whether he would find a good job played heavily on his mind.

NO BLACKS NEED HIRE

When my father arrived in England, the goal was to enroll in university, which was free at the time and to find a job. He wanted to work and send money back home to his parents as often as he could. He wasn't alone. Great Britain invited many Jamaicans and other West Indians from the Caribbean to come to England because England offered an easier way of living. Besides, due to a shortage of labor after World War II, England needed a lot of help to rebuild. Reaching out to the commonwealth colonies such as Jamaica, St. Vincent,

Barbados, etc. was only fitting.

Upon arriving in London, the cultural differences were evident. Dad's experiences were going to carry him into the unknown and the uncomfortable. England was strikingly cold, and dad remembered the wind would gush through his bones; something he wasn't used to. The presence of public bathhouses, or what some refer to as washrooms, were prevalent. These bathhouses were intended to improve the conditions of poor people in not so developed areas in London. My father was quite surprised to see how impoverished London was at the time. There were a lot of run down, abandoned houses and burned buildings. His guess was, of course a result after the war. There were many buildings left in rubbles. It was quite a contrast from the lush green landscape and tropical breeze he left behind. His expectations were built upon the idea that England was rich, and everything was perfect. The stories that were told by his teachers in Jamaica about England was contrary to what he experienced.

As confident as my father was and polite, those characteristics were not good enough to convince prospective employers to hire him. My father told me stories of knocking on doors asking for work and being told blatantly, in his face, "Sorry we don't take darkies." Or they would say, "I would like to hire you, but I cannot." One of his favorites was, "Oh, I'm sorry if you had just come by yesterday you would have gotten the job. The position is already filled." He would chuckle at that one because the intention was to unwillingly boost the ego while pulling the rug up under his feet at the same time. As dad would say, "It was a dagger to the heart." When I asked my father how he felt, he mentioned to me that at first, he didn't understand why they were referring to him as 'darkie' because his complexion was on a browner side, but once these events were happening frequently, he concluded that he was being looked at differently because of the color of his skin.

It was something he had to grapple with because in Jamaica although there was somewhat of a class structure between blacks and whites; the middle class, the upper class, it wasn't much of an overt racist society. In Jamaica, there were black policemen, black firefighters, black business owners, etc. In England at that time, there weren't any blacks in certain jobs who held those titles.

One of the first jobs my father had was at The Elgar Sheet Metal Works on Nightingale Road in the N.W. end of London. He enjoyed working there. He worked as a Welder, a craftsman. Growing up I remember seeing my father making just about anything out of metal. He would make stoves, grills, bicycle handles; just about anything. I remember thinking, "Wow, how does he know how to make these things?" Some skills he learned at Elgar, but he told me one of the very first missions he did was to go to a trade school to learn how to become a welder. Afterwards, his plan was to then attend university to study law.

Working at Elgar Sheet Metal Works gave my father the opportunity to utilize those skills he learned, and he was excited because now he was making money. Earning twelve shillings[2] a week gave him the independence and freedom to buy whatever he needed. The challenges, however, did not stray far. Dad would have to revisit the bias of other workers who would not call him by his name. They would call him Adolf. He hated being called Adolf because that was not his name. He furiously would tell them his name is Alfredo, or he would say, "You can call me Alf or Alfie but not Adolf!" They decided they would call him any name they wish, and Adolf would be the name. After a few months of working there, he accepted the fact that they were going to call him Adolf even though he cringed each time he heard the name. He never understood why they would call him such a name which to him represented suppression and dictatorship. He surmised, their disdain for the vengeful leader Hitler was being regurgitated from them, and he was going to get the brunt of it. My father thought, why should he? He's from the Caribbean.

Despite being called a name he did not like, my father looked forward to going to work. He befriended one of the workers named Leonard Collins. Leonard, an intelligent, but serious man who hardly cracked a smile, as my dad described him, would teach my father all about classical music and the other workers despised that. On one occasion when his shift was finished, Leonard called my father over towards him and told him that next week he was going to teach him about Mozart. Another worker overheard the conversation and shouted out, "Does it look like darkie needs to learn about Mozart? That's our music, not his." My father was confounded, not quite sure why this person always had something to say when Leonard would speak to him. That did not dissuade Leonard because every week Leonard taught my father something new about The Happy Black Daughter classical music. My father looked up to him. He showed my father respect and their conversations were not always centered around music, but about life in general.

With his new-found independence and now making a few shillings, my father started to feel good about his dreams and had high hopes. He was feeling great about himself. He was able to send money back home. He also enrolled in a local college. As a young nineteen-year-old man in a new but strange land far away from what was familiar, he ventured out and became acquainted with the locals and started to go out to most home parties. There weren't many clubs in London in the 1950's. There were pubs where you could go and get a couple of beers, but not necessarily dance clubs. Most of the social gatherings, especially within the West Indian communities, took place mostly in the homes of friends and neighbors.

At age 21, my father became a father to his first son, Anthony, and by the time he was 23 years of age he was the father of two boys with a young wife. At this time, dad was still working at the Elgar Sheet Metal Works but wanted additional income to supplement his family's everyday needs. He studied to become a London Black Cab driver. He took great pride in that. When we were growing up, as Children, he would always boast to us about how intense, but rewarding it was to study over 250 routes and over 20,000 points of interest needed to pass the Knowledge Exam. This is an exam covering 320 routes that

---

[2] Former English and British coin, normally valued at one-twentieth of a pound sterling, or 12 pence.

a prospective cab driver must pass in order to be a London cab driver. For some, passing the Knowledge of London exam would sometimes take two years or even longer. It was indeed a very hard exam to take. Potential cab drivers are given a scooter and a map of the city. Then they would go to various points to learn the routes. Dad would gleam with light when talking about riding his scooter around London and often getting lost on purpose, so he could find a different route. He loved being a London Black Cab driver. He made his own schedule, and the extra money was needed to support a young family.

England was offering some opportunities for dad, but with opportunity comes setbacks. Racial tension brewed plenty of violence, and protest increased in certain neighborhoods. Once driving his cab, my father saw riots between different groups. Petrol bombs, bricks, and stones were being thrown amongst the crowd. The crime was overbearing. In his mind frame, not much changed since migrating to England in 1955. In 1973, he received news that his mother in Jamaica was sick. She had fallen ill, and so off he went with his children and wife to be with his mother before she passed on.

JOURNEY'S END

The cooling evening breeze reflects

The beauty of my homeland

With rippling, winding hills surrounding peaceful

Valleys drenched with blazing sun

Far from those hills I've journeyed

Far from dear loved ones; home is my destiny; home is my aim

To hike along those sandy beaches

With sand as white as snow

The light so bright you can see for miles

Peaks and hills reaching for the clear blue sky A sky so clear, you can spot the tiniest object

Your vision allows you to

It's not too hard to reach the heights

And view beneath you, blood-tingling beauty

Looking far beyond lush green...misty valleys

Nervously, you trek among the thick vegetation

Showered by the harsh midday sun, bristling with life

It's evening now, and the sun is dying slowly

Leaving a painted sky

That no past or present painter of repute could capture

Colors numerous, no master blender could muster

That's my beautiful homeland

Darkened now is the sky

And still, the painted sky lingers

Reflecting a shimmering light

- THE HAPPY BLACK DAUGHTER -

That leaves the waters diamond studded Like rhinestones sowed on a
Paris gown

The first stars appear, and you gasp!

But soon the whole sky around you light up

With small bright stars, big stars, and distant, twinkling ones

And before you can devour this magical beauty... The moon appears

A moon that seems to be rolling off the sky

Like an orange floodlight

The moon, the painted sky, the warm, nutritious air

Beauty is for me. Beauty is the land called JAMAICA!

-Alfredo Braham

Returning to Jamaica was another transitioning period in my
father's life. He returned to the island in 1973 to be by his mother's
side to help take care of her. He then decided to stay a little longer than
he anticipated (three years to be exact) with his wife and two sons. My
father loved England because that's where he met his first wife and
became a father. He had to mature into a man rather quickly, but the
love he had for Jamaica was immeasurable. He longed for Jamaica.
Plus, he wanted to show his children where he came from. My father
knew that the same values and lessons he learned from his father had
to be passed down to his two sons. He made sure that he was present;
he had to do whatever he needed to take care of them. Also, England
at the time was still vastly reaching its racial tension peak, and dad just
didn't want to raise his children in conditions that were conducive to
racial activities. He wanted to show them a different environment that
would give them a sense of newness, and Jamaica gave them just that;
something my brothers appreciated greatly.

In Jamaica, dad became a business owner. He had a restaurant he named, African Queen, located on Manchester Street in Spanish Town. He was inspired by the movie, "The African Queen" starring Humphrey Bogart and Katherine Hepburn. There weren't many restaurants in Spanish Town in the 1970's so having a restaurant was a huge luxury, and he took great pride in that. He was a busy man figuring out how to provide for his family and most importantly, for his children. While having his own restaurant, he became a manager for the Kentucky Fried Chicken food chain in Ocho Rios. He managed other branches, at the same time helping his father, Daddy Braham in his meat shop. Building financial stability assured him that he was taking care of his children. When fathers think about raising their children, they think about how they can provide for them, how they can be better for their children and give their children what they might not have had.

Having multiple jobs to take care of the needs of his family was important for my father. Although doing so might have taken some time away from home, my father did not hesitate on spending quality time with his boys. Fishing and flying kites were some of the fun activities he enjoyed doing with my older brothers. My brothers were going to the best school, St. Jago High in Spanish Town, they were living in a modest home in Ocho Rios and life seemed more comfortable.

Can you remember a time when your father worked long hours during the week or even on the weekends? I do! Looking back, I truly appreciate the fact that my father committed to working those long hours, not because he loved it, but it contributed to his persistency. His aim to provide for his children. That is what fathers do. They show up, get to work, to pay for your school fees, pay for your school lunch, pay for that prom dress, pay the rent, and the mortgage. There's this famous line in the movie, 'To Kill a Mockingbird,' "You never really understand a person until you consider things from his point of view." I hope sons and daughters can come to an understanding that although at times you may feel like your parents are not spending enough time with you, or you're not understanding why dad may be working two, three jobs to make ends meet, understand that he's doing this for you. Understand that in his mind, he honestly does not want to let you down. He's figuring out a way to provide the best way he knows how.

What I've come to understand is that some of my father's sacrifices were made because of his selfless nature. There are a lot of fathers who are making selfless decisions every day; those decisions are almost always for the benefit of their children. I can say some of my father's life decisions brought some challenges, but it also brought a lot of blessings.

THE HAPPY WITHIN YOU CHALLENGE

Can you think of a time when your father sacrificed for you? What can you acknowledge and celebrate about your father's sacrifices?

······· 2 ·······
OH, BLESS THIS CHILD!

I believe that every father wants to have a daughter as much as they want to have a son. It's only natural for a father to want to have a son to carry on his namesake and feel proud. The males in my family surely do. Having a girl is just as amazing; it changes everything. Fathers gain a different perspective from their daughters and develop more of an appreciation towards women. Daughters allow fathers to realize that one day she will become a woman so they are more responsive to their daughter's needs than they would be to their sons. An article by Jennifer Mascaro was published in the American Psychological Association regarding this. According to Dr. Mascaro, "Most dads are trying to do the best they can and do all the things they can to help their kids succeed, but it's important to understand how their interactions with their children might be subtly biased based on gender.3" After speaking with Dr. Mascaro, I concluded that this was very true.

When my mother was pregnant with me, my father told her that if the baby was a girl, he would make sure she would never have to struggle again. He would lift her out of anything that was negative. I asked my mother what happened when I was born. The day my father found out that I was a girl he told my mother, "You have made me the happiest man on earth." Spanish Town Hospital in Jamaica had the most elated man inside that ward. December 30, 1979 was a day my father would never forget. His angel was born, and life with her would be a journey they both would treasure.

---

3 Child Gender Influences Paternal Behavior, Language, and Brain Function, Jennifer S. Mascaro, PhD, Patrick D. Hackett, BS, and James K. Rilling, PhD, Emory University; Kelly E. Rentscher, PhD, and Matthias R. Mehl, PhD, University of Arizona; Behavioral Neuroscience.

- THE HAPPY BLACK DAUGHTER -

Oh, bless this joyous birth

And bless this mother's worth

And bless this father's oats so wild Oh, bless this dear sweet child.

(Written December 1979)

-Alfredo Braham, Memoirs in Poetry 2014

I came into my father's life during a period where he was getting back on his feet. He was still working in his restaurant and managing one of the chain restaurants, Kentucky Fried Chicken, along with my grandfather's meat shop. However, there were challenges running a small business. He also had to worry about family members stealing from the business, so it became very hard to support me as a young child. When the meat shop went out of business, dad had no choice but to find another job working at, Alkali Salt, a factory in Spanish Town where he became a foreman (his brother had sold the business behind my father's back and convinced my grandfather, now blind, to sign the papers to sell the business). It was a blow to him and to my grandfather. However, dad persisted. He never gave up. He became such a dominant leader while working at the factory. Dad was a leader at home and a strong leader at work. While at Alkali, he advocated for the company to offer 3 weeks paternity leave for new fathers, and they did.

Food in all cultures connect and brings people together in a way that demonstrates love. When it came to food, my father enjoyed the entire process. He did most of the cooking in the household.

He loved cooking. He loved preparing it, and he loved sharing it. As an infant, breast milk was not my specialty, but I favored dad's infamous pumpkin soup and cornmeal porridge.

---

published May 22, 2017.

https://www.apa.org/news/press/releases/2017/05/fathersdaughters

A visit from the milk man brought excitement and thrill as he would deliver farm fresh, delicious milk. Yes, there were still milkmen making home deliveries of fresh milk back in the late 70's and 80's in Jamaica, a tradition that has left the island for the most part, unless you raise your own cows and have access to your own fresh, organic milk.

As a man, dad's number one priority was to take care of his family. He prided himself on making sure food was on the table, and the environment for his family was safe. Our family ritual was a walk in the park, a stroll to the local shops, then on to get ice-cream from Creamy Corner on Wellington Street in Spanish Town. But, going to church proceeded these events. Although my father was not a religious man, and hardly went to church, as children we never missed a day. Similarly, to his upbringing as a child where his parents made sure Sunday was the day of worship and gratitude.

As a toddler, my father's escape from my presence was forbidden. Any attempt to exit my sight would create a wailing, lamented, bawl of which my neighbors suffered the consequence. My cries would simmer down once my father picked me up, walked me outside, then propped me up on one of the columns on the fence. A little kiss on the cheek and a gentle wiping away of my tears soothed my whimpering. Ah, a father's love!

Who says fathers aren't changing diapers and cooking for their children? I believe that old tale is long gone. Now, I can say most men prefer not to change diapers, due to not being able to withstand the stench that launches out at them. The thought of the sticky fecal matter cemented between the creases of a baby's bump can present a queasy feeling for most dads. One thing I must say is that fathers have been cleaning their children's bottom for centuries. When my father was born, my grandfather Egbert on many occasions would bathe and clean him. He would then pass him on to his mother to get clothed. Before my father's birth, his grandfather, John Richmond Vidal Braham would cook for his son. That was in the 19th century.

When I think about the relationship a father has with his children, I think about the willingness of the father. Fathers are willing to do what is right to ensure their children are taken care of. My grandfather was prepared, and my father was willing. My great-grandfather was willing.

WASHING THE NAPPIES

One eventful morning in Jamaica my father woke up mistakenly thinking it was later than it was. The shimmering, glossy moonlight had given off a bright glazing sheen, in which my father thought was daylight. He remembered there were some nappies of mine in the basin that needed to be washed. He ousted himself out of bed and went outside to the backyard where the standpipe was to catch water. As the sleep dissipated from his eyes, he started to become fully aware and realized it was still night outside. He thought about going back to bed but decided since he was already up, he would stay up with the moonlight.

My mother at the time was away at her grand uncle's funeral, so dad was left to take care of me for the weekend. In the glistening moonlight, in good old fashion tradition, he gathered together some wood to make the fire outside and a pot of water. While waiting for the water to boil, he prepared the container for the first step of the washing process. The first step was to wash the nappies in cold water using the blue cake soap, a typical laundry detergent that is often used by most Jamaicans. After washing the nappies with the blue cake soap and giving them a good rinse, he put the nappies into the boiling water. Boiling nappies is very common. The process helps to strip away any extra contaminates lodged within the cloth like material. Dad repeated these steps a few times as there were a lot of nappies to be washed and boiled. Hearing a little noise in the yard, a neighbor looked over the fence and asked, "Mr. Braham, a weh yuh a do?"

"What are you doing?" She asked him.

With a chuckle, my father replied, "I'm doing a little washing."

"Mr. Braham, yuh wake up early fi wash yuh daughter clothes? A still nighttime. What a proud puppa yuh is?" She said in her Jamaican Patois. "Oh, yes, I'm very proud. I didn't realize it was still night, but the job has to be done."

He washed, boiled, and hung the nappies on the line, waiting for that crispy sunlight to hover over them so they could dry. The next day, the neighbor went outside in her backyard looking over the fence admiring the bright white nappies. She then went around the community talking about how Mr. Rue (dad's nickname) washed his daughter's nappies, and how he didn't have to wait on Miss Dorcas (my mother) to do it.

When I think about how simple acts such as bathing, cooking and being present helps to cultivate a strong bond between parent and child, it makes me smile. My heart overflows with great admiration for parents who are doing simple activities with their children and for their children. I applaud those fathers, black fathers in particular, who have challenged the myth of the "invisible dad." The truth of the matter is black fathers have been taking care of their children for centuries. According to a report by the Center for Disease Control (CDC), and a recent study by Dr. Travis L. Dixon., "It is a dangerous distortion to Black families to incorrectly depict Black fathers as uninvolved or not present in the lives of their children, thereby, inaccurately suggesting that Black fathers are absent and abandon their children, especially given there is a lack of evidence to support those claims."

My father washing my nappies, cooking for me, walking me to the park, and taking me to school wasn't something he thought of doing because he wanted to defy the myth. These were innate acts; they were his responsibility as a father. I cannot remember a time when my father was not there for me. He showed up in so many ways, and so have other amazing black fathers. They too are showing up for their daughters, for their children. That old wives' tale is far from the truth.

GUN SHOTS, HIGH FEVER!

In the election year of 1980, Kingston, Jamaica was plagued by a political upheaval between the People's National Party and the Jamaica Labour Party. In Spanish Town, heavy gunshots and brutal killings were happening just about every night. Even in broad daylight gangs were involved in gun battle. One night I was stricken by a high fever; my eyes were rolled back into their sockets, and my body was limp. In the midst of the exchange of gunfire throughout the city, my mother feared rushing me to the hospital. When the home remedies didn't seem to work, my mother had no choice but to rush me to the hospital. Walking in the night for my mother was walking into the unknown.

A neighbor accompanied her to what seemed to be the longest walk to the hospital. Spanish Town Hospital was a 2 mile walk away. The nurses laid me inside a large bucket with ice cold water with tiny pieces of ice cubes. My mother said my head could not stay on my body as it was feeble and shaky. My body felt like hot asphalt. I stayed in the hospital for an entire week, submerged in ice cold bucket of water. Once my father found out, the first thing he wanted to do was to make a big pot of pumpkin soup, and that's exactly what he did. Every day he cooked my favorites: pumpkin soup and cornmeal porridge. When I came out of the hospital, the cooking continued, and the role was now reversed; he would not leave my sight. My mother's love and attention soothed me, but daddy's love was just as beautiful and gentle to the touch.

Growing up in Jamaica in the 80's was a period of political changes and with political changes came economic changes. The financial debt of the 1980s increased to a sky-high rate and affected many Jamaicans. The one thing, however, that was not affected by the economic change was my father's love. His love did not decrease even during the trying times.

Dad made sure that as children we enjoyed the simple pleasures of life. His greatest and best teachings were through nature. There were many visits to the beach and the zoo. There was also fishing trips, road trips to the countryside where we visited family. At times we pulled over at the side of the road to pick up mangos from off the ground which had fallen from the trees. I remember each time we would pass a mango tree, I would get so excited. I would always shout out, "Daddy, pull ova, pull ova. Let's pick some mangos." Dad would get out the car and start by shaking the trees so some of the mangos would fall onto the ground. Off we went, climbing mango trees.

Me, my dad, my brother Eddie would pick them and pass them to the wide receiver, my mom. We picked so many mangos that we had to give some away along our journey. There were the stringy mangoes, the Number 11 mangos, and then my favorite, the Julie Mango. In the end, dad made sure the biggest of mangos were always mine, something I took pleasure in. While I rave about having the biggest of mangos, my mother and brother's jealousy did not surface because it was the smallest ones that were the sweetest.

One of the most important things I believe a father can do is to spend time with his children because those memorable experiences between father and child will be a long-lasting memory. There are many lessons to be learned from those experiences. Looking back at our road trip, I learned not to be afraid to climb a mango tree, or any tree for that matter because I saw my father climbing the mango tree. I learned that when you have more than enough, share some with others. Most importantly, I learned the attention that was given to me by my father that day made me feel so happy and loved.

If you are a father reading this book, what memorable experiences have you given your children? I ask this question because I know there are a lot of fathers who might feel like in order to give your child a memorable experience you must have a lot of money to do so, but all children need is your abiding attention. That involves simple, basic activities. I know that was what I craved from my father. Just him being there was enough for me.

UP, UP, AND AWAY!

Funny how life would have it, 30 years prior, it was my father's curiosity for life that led him to a foreign land. Fate would have it that my father wanted to do the same thing for me too. He wanted to bring me to a different environment, so I would have a different experience like he did when he left Jamaica to travel to England.

I remember one night as a child sitting on the steps in front of my house in Jamaica. I looked up in the sky and imagined this foreign land my father and mother would often speak about. I imagined this foreign land existing among the clouds as a majestic wonderland that had golden roads. Everything there was wonderful. Whenever I was in church, and I heard the pastor talk about the heavens are among the clouds, I often wondered if he was talking about 'foreign.' Was 'foreign' heaven? Foreign is a word most Jamaicans use to describe America or any country that was not Jamaica. The word foreign means: distant, overseas something not familiar to your native environment. We would say, "We're going to foreign" or "She just got back from foreign."

In the mindset of some people in Jamaica that word 'foreign' seems to mean something better, greater than the environment they are living in; like how my grandfather and father thought about England. There was something that England had that Jamaica didn't have. Towards the late 70's and early 80's there was a resurgence of Jamaicans fleeing their island sun for a better environment. There was something that 'foreign' had that Jamaica didn't have.

I was elated the day I found out I was going to 'foreign.' A trip to the phone booth one Sunday evening sparked excitement and thrill. I trekked alongside my mother holding her hands as we walked down the bent, curved road. My excitement grew when I finally saw the two phone booths, one of which was marked by bullet holes and the other had no glass screen to protect the circumference of the phone. I couldn't wait to get inside because on the other end of the receiver was my father. I heard my mother ask my father about the necessary papers needed to take to the embassy. Being so young I did not know what an embassy was. All I knew was that I wanted to see my father. However, the way my father answered my mom must have been quite a relief because she reacted with a huge smile then a boisterous laugh. "She's right here," my mother said.

I knew that meant he was asking for me, and I gleamed with delight to speak with him.

Whenever my father spoke to me, it was always in a gentle, soft-spoken and soothing tone. It was different compared to how he spoke to my brothers. Even throughout adulthood, he spoke in a delicate, not too high pitch with a hint of that British accent. He had left Jamaica to go to New York 3 months prior and started working at a major construction company once again, working as a foreman. I asked my father when I was going to see him. He explained to me that I would see him soon and that I'll be leaving Jamaica to be with him and the rest of his family in America. I knew that I was going to leave behind friends and family, but the one thing my father did was reassure me that change is good sometimes.

One thing for sure about fathers is that they are always looking for ways to make things better for their children. His decision to have his family migrate to a different country for a better life had a direct impact on me. When I look back, I realize that my father created a life around the things he valued most, and that was family. He might not have gotten a lot of things right, (no father is perfect) but his core beliefs in which he demonstrated was based on these three words:

1. **Providing:** He provided emotional, financial support even when times were not the best financially, his emotional presence stood abound.

2. **Protecting:** He protected his children by fostering a strong bond, so they can later protect themselves.

3. **Producing:** He was the creator of his life whose responsible and competent actions produced results.

Those results helped to strengthen his children. My father decided to uproot his family and bring them to a new environment because it was his fatherly instinct to provide for his family. It was his fatherly instinct that wanted to continue to protect us from any form of struggle and harm. It was not just his fatherly instinct, but it was vital for him to create a space where we as children felt safe and where the sky was the limit, where opportunities are endless.

BRIGHT LIGHTS, BIG CITY

Imagine your head bobbing and weaving back and forth right now. Your shoulders are relaxed, and you're either sitting down or standing up leaning against a door, or you might be laying down in bed reading this or at a coffee shop. Start moving your head back and forth and have fun with it while you begin to read these hip-hop words out loud:

Welcome to the melting pot

Corners where we selling rock

Afrika Bambaataa sh*t

Home of the hip-hop

Yellow cab, gypsy cab, dollar cab, holla back For foreigners it ain't fair they act like they forgot how to act

Eight million stories out there in the naked

City, it's a pity half of y'all won't make it

Me I gotta plug Special Ed, "I got it made"

If Jesus payin' LeBron, I'm payin' Dwayne Wade

Three dice Cee-lo Three-card Monte

Labor Day parade, rest in peace Bob Marley Statue of Liberty long
live the World Trade Long live the king yo!

I'm from the Empire State that's... In New York

-Jay Z.[4]

Now, if you were moving with a beat in your head while reading
that above, I hope it sounded like that of Jay Z's version because for me
that is what I hear in my head when I think about being on the plane
March 1988 flying high in the sky going to 'foreign.'

---

[4]Jay Z. Empire State of Mind, the Blueprint 3 Album 2009

THE HAPPY WITHIN YOU CHALLENGE

Think of a time when your father made a decision that impacted your life for the better? What was that and how can you show gratitude for that decision?

I SAID YES, THEN I SAID NO

My father gave me the biggest advice on love and relationship. It took me by surprise because I thought when it came to topics such as dating, sex, and love, he would be a bit apprehensive to speak on these topics, especially to his daughter. To discuss such issues would make the uncomfortable even more uncomfortable. When he did speak on this, however, it was such a warm revelation, and it gave me solace at a time when I needed to be reassured.

The fall of 2004 was an exciting time because I was studying hard for my finals and needed to pass my classes in order to graduate. Graduating college would be the most gratifying experience for me. I knew how important it was for my parents to see me accomplish this amazing milestone, and I did not want to let them down. I could not wait to make them proud. The events leading up to graduation were exciting, fun, and confusing. It was hard work, and I knew it would all be worth it. I wanted to buckle down and hit the books to ensure I graduated. Nothing would stop me. There would be no distractions to sway me away from making myself and my parents proud.

There was a point where studying became so strenuous. I remember one night being so tired my eyes were swollen from reading. My hands were hurting me so bad from typing on my Gateway desktop computer for hours on end. I felt so empowered sitting in front of my computer typing away, researching for my reports. It gave me a feeling of importance. My father would make me a cup of tea and walk over to me and say, "That's my girl. Here you go, my daughter."

He would hand me a hot cup of Lipton tea with carnation milk and sugar in it, along with a big smile on his face. I was exhausted, but I was determined to finish the task.

I remember waking up the next morning still sitting in front of the computer with my head hung over towards the back of the chair. I looked around seeing nothing but books upon books, papers all over the room. I said to myself, "Wow this final semester at Brooklyn College is brutal." As I was getting up from the chair, I unexpectedly received a phone call from one of my friends who invited me out that evening. As much as I wanted to stay in the house and keep on studying, I really needed to let my hair down, and a night out on the town with the girls seemed to be a good idea.

My friends know me well. They know anything that has to do with music, I'll be there. Music brings out the fun, silly side of me. If I ever became too silly and engrossed in music, they would pretend as if they didn't know me. Their selective memory would kick in. Ally who? The cold fall evening almost changed my decision to go out that night, but I caved in. You know, those friends, the ones who will peer pressure you regardless of your reluctance to anything. Well, off I went to have some fun and loosen up the brain cells a little with two of my besties.

It was the typical club scene. The taxi pulled up to the LAB, a Brooklyn nightclub that was known for some good vibes and known to have popular guest artists. The queue to get in was halfway around the other side of the building. I dreaded standing outside in the cold. It was in that moment where I looked at Vaneisha and Crystal and asked, "So, do either one of you know a guy that knows a guy who can get us in?" It was frigid cold. I had on no leggings, just a simple leather skirt with boots and a red 'pleather' jacket aka fake leather. The thought of waiting in queue for a long time gave me anxiety. We had no choice but to huddle together until we were close enough to get inside. Right before I felt like I was going to pass out, I noticed this guy who looked familiar to me. I elbowed Crystal and asked her if she remembered this guy who was a club promoter and performer. We both looked at each and immediately knew exactly who he was. We knew he knew a guy, who knew a guy, that could let us in. It turned out that he was the guy to let us inside. Alex was a club promoter who also hosted parties at the Lab every week.

"Hey Alex," I shouted out his name and waved at him to get his attention. While he crossed the street towards the front of the queue, I ran up as nicely as I could. I remembered my legs feeling numb at this point. My fingers felt like they were about to fall off and break into little pieces. Alex saw me and remembered me from a couple of the parties he threw in Bedford Stuyvesant and Crown Heights. "Hey, Ally B what's going on Queen?" I answered with a polite smile, "I'm doing great. Hey, uh you think you can let me and two of my friends inside as your guests?" I did not waste any time asking him. It was a brick city out there, and I wanted to get inside! Alex without hesitation replied, "What ya mean... of course. Where they at?" in true New York twang, and boom we were in.

It was that Snoop Dog song, "Drop It Like It's Hot" that propelled me on the dance floor. My stone-cold legs started to feel like a hot tamale. They were warming up alright. I found myself lost in the bliss of the music as Vaneisha and Crystal presented me with a glass of Baileys (one of the only liquors I order from a bar, maybe Long Island Iced Tea as well). While taking a sip of the Bailey's, I feel a gentle touch on the shoulder which snapped me back into reality. I turned around, and it was a tall guy, broad shoulders and not so bad looking from what I could see in the glaring club lights. He asked me for a dance, and before I gave him an answer, I looked at him once more, this time up and down, to see if he looked at least decent and approachable. I said, "Sure!" He was polite enough to ask for a dance compared to other guys who usually push themselves against you from behind without your permission. We ladies don't appreciate that.

The dance between Terence and I made me forget I was even with my girls that night. It was an electric chemistry I did not expect to happen, and It felt great! After the dance, he gave me his number, but he did not ask me for mine. He simply said, "Give me a call, I want to take you out." I thought it was interesting that he didn't ask me for my number but in my head, I assumed he was being respectful or wanted to be chased.

We left the club in the wee hours of the morning. Vaneisha, Crystal, and I enjoyed ourselves so much we were too tired to walk up and down Fulton Street to look for a cab. All three of us decided not to drive that night but, we managed to flag down a cab.

It was Sunday morning, the day after the club. I felt rejuvenated. Sundays are days that I cherish because for me, it is a day of relaxation and meditation. When you put in the work, you should always reward yourself. You should not be afraid to let your hair down. I turned on the music. I watched a couple of movies. Anything to feel good besides a little fun and play is needed sometimes. That expression "Work hard, play hard" holds true.

I couldn't wait to get back to studying and tackle the semester. I was spending a lot of time in Boylan Hall. It felt like the closer it was to take my finals, the more intense studying became. I had my media studies class and my math studies class. I had an African studies paper that was fifteen pages long. At the time, seemed impossible to write. It was a lot to do. I felt overwhelmed. I needed to figure out a way to hunker down and not feel so alone with this process.

Some classmates started a study group, which I thought was a great idea to be a part of because I needed the support. We often tend to think that we can do everything by ourselves and because of that we don't reach out for help. I used to be that girl. I used to have this limiting belief that I'm not good in group settings. I rather work by myself. Or I would say, "I'm resourceful enough to find my way." The truth is we cannot do it alone. The study group was exactly what I needed.

After our first meet up, one of the members of the group invited us to a Halloween party that weekend. I immediately thought, "There's no way I'll go out again, two weekends in a row when I'm supposed to be studying. I don't even celebrate Halloween." The last time I dressed up for Halloween I was ten years old. After saying, "No," I was pulled to the side by one of the group members who reminded me about my favorite quote, "Work hard, Play hard." I thought about it, and once again, I caved in. I agreed I would be at the party.

While leaving campus I thought about calling Terence to invite him. I wanted to call him, and I didn't want to call him. I thought maybe it was too soon to call him. After all, it had only been four days since meeting him. "Maybe I shouldn't wait so long to call him. He might have forgotten about me," I thought. But the thought that he didn't ask for my number bothered me, and I wanted to know why, so I decided to call him.

Our conversation started with us revisiting the weekend before at the club. Terence had a smooth, mellow toned voice. It wasn't high. It wasn't low. It was just in between the two. We talked for about an hour before I invited him to the Halloween party. He agreed, and I was really looking forward to it. Now all I had to do was to figure out what costume I would wear. I decided my costume of choice would be the Queen of Sheba costume. I remember it being this gold and white color and of course it came with a crown. As I've mentioned before, I'm not the one to dress up in costumes and parade myself around for Halloween, but I do get great pleasure in seeing children's faces light up when candy is being distributed. Candy just makes things better don't you think?

I was a little nervous meeting up with Terrence, but I wanted to see if we still had that spark between us and possibly see where that would lead. After an hour or so waiting on him, in comes Terrence as Darryl McDaniel's from Run DMC. The hat, the gold chain, the black bomber jacket, he had the whole gear on. Well, almost the whole gear. As I looked down towards his feet, I could not believe what I saw! I was in shock! Looking puzzled, He asked me, "What's wrong?"

"Where are the Adidas?" I asked him.

"What?" He asked.

"If you are going to represent RUN DMC, you must wear Adidas sneakers." I was adamant about that; it's only respect. We both laughed. Although I was teasing him about not wearing Adidas sneakers, at least I saw that his love for hip-hop and music was something we both shared, and that was a plus.

After a couple of hours at the party, Terrence signaled me that he wanted to leave. I thought, "why not"? This kind of party wasn't my cup of tea anyway. Off we went to get ice cream at the McDonalds on Court Street. What I cannot forget was how a couple of the staff were staring at us. We assumed it was due to our dress code which might have intrigued them. I didn't care because I thought I was the best-looking Queen of Sheba ever!

As we sat down, I noticed Terence did not pull out the chair for me, which I thought was bad manners in general, but more importantly, a Queen never pulls out her own chair to sit down. I didn't bother to draw that to his attention. I made a mental note that if the next time we should meet in such a setting, he had better demonstrate how a queen should be treated. The chair needs to be pulled out then gently ushered under the table. Terence and I were very talkative. He also had what we Jamaicans would call: sweet mouth.

"Him 'ave sweet mout."

Words were coming out of his mouth like a cascading waterfall; it was plentiful and quick. He leaned over to me and poured into me how he thought I would make an excellent wife and the mother of his children. His delectable pleasantries presented itself to be somewhat fascinating, and I indulged in every bit of it. The way he described my figure was as if Rembrandt was painting his last best piece of art; exquisitely done. After he exhausted all he could, I proceeded to explain to him that although I am utterly flattered and smitten by his charm, my focus is to graduate college and my studies are important to me. He proclaimed that he understood quite well, and he would wait until after graduation so we can get married. I was perplexed by this because I just met him a week ago and here he is discussing marriage. I insisted, however, that what I wanted at that time was a friend who would unselfishly support me in all my endeavors and to just have fun with. He thought it was all jokes. He laughed but assured me that whatever I wanted was what he wanted. I must confess; his charm provoked a curiosity. I was intrigued.

I arrived home tired. I spent half an hour looking for parking as dad's car was parked up in the driveway. I finally walked inside at around 2:30 am, couldn't wait to get in the bed but dreaded the fact that I would have to dethrone myself from my royal ornaments. Once the costume was removed, the Queen of the East was ready for her slumber. I settled in nicely until I heard a knock on my bedroom door.

My father was waiting for me downstairs. I wasn't sure if something was wrong if there was an emergency of some sort. I reluctantly opened the door. Feeling concerned I asked him if he was okay?

He replied, "Yes, I need to talk to you right now."

My heart skipped a beat because I hadn't heard that tone in his voice in a long time, so I reckoned he was serious.

"You've been spending a lot of time gallivanting, around haven't you?"

The look on my father's face said it all. He was upset, and when my father is upset, you are going to hear it. I, of course, begged to differ. I thought in my head, "A lot of time gallivanting?" I was a bit puzzled. "What do you mean by that"? I knew what gallivanting meant, but I wanted him to explain himself. In good old-fashioned tone he said to me, "You know exactly what I mean."

He continued with this lengthy monologue which I really wasn't interested in hearing because all I wanted to do was go to bed, but I had no choice but to listen. "Allison, Allison (when my name is called twice, this means it's serious as a heart attack). Now, I want you to listen to me good. I've been observing you lately, worrying about your final exams. I've heard you complaining about how difficult this semester is for you, and I've watched you throw your books down in frustration just because you were tired. I am not going to stand by and allow my daughter to be partying every chance she gets when her whole future is dependent on this graduation coming up. You have an obligation to yourself my dear to buckle up and stay on the path. No daughter of mine is going to throw away her dreams. You are going to get serious about this studying young lady. All this partying has to stop. You hear me?"

His animated finger pointed exuberantly in the air while I flinched because I didn't know where it was going to land. And just when I thought he was finished, and I was about to tell him that I was not going to throw away anything, he continued. "You are a young lady, and there is nothing wrong with going out, but you got to know when to appear and when to disappear. You had no business staying out so long knowing well that you have to clamp down on your studies."

As the tears stream down my face as I write this paragraph, I couldn't help but remember how my father looked in his face. I could see the passion in his eyes, and I sensed a little bit of quilt in his tone of voice. My father never finished college. He never became the lawyer he wanted to become. He didn't become Johnny Cochran, but in my eyes, he became so many other great things. Perhaps, he would have been a unique kind of lawyer. He would have had his own gleeful style with a strong gravitas demeanor. However, I knew one thing he did not want was his daughter to go down that same path. I had to listen to daddy dearest even at the grown age of twenty-four. I wasn't too old to get a lecture.

My father knew how important education was, and although he did not finish college, he was exposed to it. He didn't allow not completing college to prevent him from learning. The school of life was his college where he learned many lessons. The newspaper, book clubs, poetry clubs, his interactions with people from all walks of life, those were his teachers. My dad took it upon himself to read almost every day whether it was the newspaper, Shakespeare, Robert Burns, James Baldwin, Cunty Cullen, Bernard Shaw, or Edgar Allan Poe to name a few. He surrounded himself with people whose intelligence was wise beyond their years.

AND JUST LIKE THAT, FINALS WEEK CAME!

I was so nervous and couldn't wait to get it over with. On the eve before I had to turn in my African Studies paper, I decided to take another look to review the report and make any necessary changes to ensure it was just right. Dad took it upon himself to assist me in that effort. He was that anchor who guided and helped with my understanding of the African Diaspora. He poured into me the tales of Kwame Nkrumah's relentless work towards an independent and modern Ghana. My father went on telling me about his encounter with Geoffrey Bing, who was a British Barrister, and Attorney General of Ghana under Nkrumah. He met Geoffrey Bing one evening in London as a taxi driver. He picked him and his young son up from the airport.

Their conversation led my father to invite Mr. Bing to his home for dinner. Bing at the time had no choice but to return to London after Nkrumah was ousted as president in 1966 and he had to reestablish himself back into the political limelight of England. Removed by the opposition leaders, a coup d'état[5], he returned to London with a young adopted son from Ghana with no clarity as to how his career as a Barrister was going to be. During their conversation over dinner, my father told me that he learned so much about what Bing and Nkrumah did together for what he believed to be for the betterment of Ghana. As dinner was winding down, Geoffrey Bing promised my father he would revisit him next time with a copy of his book he was working on called "Reap the Whirlwind."

When I looked at my report, I thought about how I could add this amazing new-found information my father was sharing with me. After all, I wanted to brag about my father's encounter with a political revolutionary who helped to change the trajectory of a nation. Not to mention I became even more excited once my father showed me the autographed book of "Reap the Whirlwind." It was penned, "To Alfred, in appreciation of his kindness to our family." I eventually referenced Ghana as one of the first British colonies in the African continent to gain independence from the hands of colonialism.

My father was always teaching me, and he was aware of his teaching moments with me. If he wasn't teaching me verbally, he would storm into my room or wherever I was and hand me a book to read. He was always encouraging me to read. This was his way of saying, "If you don't know the answer to something, seek it and you shall find it." The answers are always there.

---

[5] Coup d'etat: Also called a Coup, the sudden, violent, illegal seizure of power from a government.

THE PROPOSAL: A FOOL FOR LOVE

Most of us, at one point in our lives, have gotten into a situation where we thought the person who was meant for us was going to save us. They were going to complete us and make us whole. But when reality hits, you find that kind of thinking was just a complete farce. My infatuation, in which I later learned was infatuation, not love, with Terrence contributed to a whirlwind of emotions within me. It was really hard to contain, but that experience gave me a better understanding of knowing who I am, what I want, and to never be blinded by what I believe to be love ever again.

A week before I found out whether I passed my exams I was spending a lot of time with Terrence. We went shopping. We spent many evenings having deli sandwiches, pizza and some evenings, I managed to thrust myself into his kitchen to make his favorite, oxtail with rice and peas. He wanted to be with a woman who could cook "good West Indian food." Terrence was not from Jamaica but from the Caribbean so, we both shared the same cultural love for great authentic Caribbean cuisine. My best year was coming into fruition! I was about to graduate and make my parents proud. I was also dating someone who wined and dined me, and I felt great.

My trip to campus was a rewarding one. Terrence escorted me and waited patiently for me in the student lounge as I learned that I had passed all my finals, qualifying me to walk down that graduation aisle. What do you do when the feeling of joy overwhelms you? You jump for joy! It was an exuberant feeling to know that all my hard work paid off. I could not wait to share the news with my family, especially to my counsel in chief, my dad. Walking back to the car, Terrence was excited and wanted to celebrate by having a bite to eat. I wanted to get back home to share the news with family, so we opted for hot dogs from one of the hot dog street vendors. As we were waiting for our hot dogs, I noticed someone staring at Terrence from across the street. She was a much older lady with a heavy-set body type. She crossed over and approached us, then turned to Terrence and asked him if this was his new hobby. By "this" she was referring to me.

I saw how uncomfortable he was, but more importantly, I wanted to know who the woman was. After questioning Terrence, he informed me that she was the mother of his ex-girlfriend, and she was just jealous of seeing him moving on. I was taken aback because why would she use the word "hobby". A hobby is something that is done frequently for pleasure, for fun and you enjoy doing it. The thought of me being a hobby lodged in my brain for weeks, and I couldn't get it out of my head.

After the encounter, I hadn't seen Terrence for two weeks. He did not call me. I called him, but he would not pick up his phone. Finally, after weeks had passed, I received a phone call saying it was because he was busy working long hours, he was tired after work, and that was the reason he didn't pick up his phone. Plus, he told me he was working on a surprise and couldn't wait to share it with me over dinner. His explanation did not sit well with me, but I gave him the benefit of the doubt. Women are naturally intuitive creatures, so although my intuition told me something was not right, I shook it off because women are also easy to be forgiving.

Since we both loved to indulge in the art of eating, the time came for him to take me out to dinner. It was a windy, chilly, but beautiful fall evening in Brooklyn. I remember when I came out of the car. I couldn't wait to get inside the warm, cozy restaurant as the breeze was blowing so harshly, and my hooded coat was fighting against the wind. We both loved Caribbean food, but that night we opted for Italian. Those Olive Garden breadsticks were calling my name. He pulled out the chair for me, and as we sat down, I noticed he was sweating. He kept clasping the palm of his hands together. I was curious to know what was on his mind, but not so fast. A girl needed to eat first.

Eventually, as I was finishing my second round of sangria, he excused himself from the table. He barely finished his Shrimp Scampi. This time when he came back to the table the sweat seemed as if it was seeping through his sweater. Terrence reached for my hand and began to talk about how marriage was important to him, and he would make me the happiest woman. He even went as far as telling me we could adopt children if I wanted to. Once again, I was a bit surprised.

I did not understand why he was bent on getting married so quickly. Before I could allow my brain to understand what he was saying entirely, there was a loud applause and cheer coming from some of the staff members who walked over with two slices of chocolate mousse cake adorned with candles. They approached the table clapping and cheering, while Terrence, looking like a lost sheep with his sweater at this point drenched with sweat, reached over to touch my hand then asked me without kneeling, "Will you marry me?"

My mouth dropped opened, my heart felt like it was coming out of my chest and my stomach was bubbling and making all sorts of sounds. This felt odd to me, I froze. My brain could not process all of this. I quickly played in my head the fact that I was about to graduate, I told myself that I love him, and we can make it work. After all, he was handsome, charming and a hard worker. I remember throwing my head back and smilingly and chuckled as I said. "Oh, my God. Yes!" In my head I was thinking, "Did I just say yes?" I told myself that this was what growing up was all about. I was making grown-up decisions. All the stars were lining up for me. Graduation and a great paying job was around the corner. A hard-working, handsome man was staring right in front of me. I told myself that he was going to provide and take care of me, and I believed it. I asked my 24-year-old self, "How could I allow this to slip away from me?" I didn't want to.

ARE YOU SERIOUS? WAKE UP, GIRL!

Now was the time to share the news with my parents. That evening I explained to Terrence he would have to meet with them, and he agreed. I knew this would be a shock to them, but I also knew that this was the opportunity to show them that everything was falling into place. I'm graduating, I'm going to get a great job, and I'm going to have a husband to share that with me and take care of me. Everything sounded great until I spoke with my father and mother around the dinner table one evening. They both laughed so hard at my breaking news. They were not convinced. The fact that Terrence had not met them created an even more of an uneasiness, especially for my father. One of the first things my mother asked me was, "What does he want from you?" In her flamboyant Jamaican flare, she said, "Mind him want to marry you to get a green card." I was distraught, and I remember feeling as if they weren't taking me seriously.

While I was upset at my parents laughing at the situation, I understood why. They hadn't met Terrence. I was not presented with a ring. Nope. You read that right. Terrence did not have a ring when he asked me to marry him. Also, as the weeks went by, he had different reasons as to why he was unable to meet my father. This made me confused, suspicious and nervous. I began to think about all the times I had to meet up with Terrence. He would only come to pick me up in the evenings and would wait outside. As a giddy young lady, I didn't realize how obscure that was.

About three weeks after the proposal, I was sitting around my computer checking my email when I received a call from a woman who was breathing profusely over the phone. I answered, "Who is this?" She replied by calling my first name and began to tell me that she was Terrence girlfriend. In disbelief, I laughed and hung up the phone only for it to ring again. This time she sounded calm and started to explain to me that I was just a placeholder for Terrence. She said to me that she was in a relationship with him, but she had traveled overseas for a few months, and now that she is back, I needed to take a backseat. If ever there was a moment that would confirm my doubts, anxiety, and my parents' nonchalant attitude towards this 'proposal,' this would be it. At that moment, I felt a dark cloud hover over me. The room went black, and all my organs were looking for an escape route. The feeling of guilt, shame and disbelief overwhelmed me. Then came the rage. The rage came once I heard Terrence's voice in the background shouting and arguing as he tried to defend himself. I will be doing you as a reader an injustice if I fail to mention that I did use a lot of expletives. I'll allow you to imagine what some of those words were.

Once I crouched down unto the floor and cried my eyes out, I thought about why I was such a fool to think this kind of artificial love was real. All this time he was with someone else. I asked myself so many questions and blamed myself for my lack of emotional intelligence. Why didn't I recognize the lies coming from his mouth? Everything looked good on the surface but hollow, cold and ugly from the inside. What's a girl to do? All the way through the end of December, I didn't want to do anything. I was angry and hurt. All I wanted to do was eat, sleep and stay in my own space for the rest of the winter. I didn't want friends to come around or call me. I wanted none of that.

My father had had enough of my sad behavior, so one day he summoned me to the living room. Being careful not to flare up my anger and send me back to my secluded space, he gently gestured towards the coffee table. On the table was a cup of tea with some Shirley biscuits. He then said, "Sit down." in his soft-spoken tone. I knew a long monologue with passionate words was going to come out. He started by taking in a deep breath. He raised his arm and pointed his index finger in the air and began... "You know Allison, you're a young lady, and I cannot tell you who you should date and who you shouldn't date. I can only tell you to use your head and your heart.

Go with your heart first because that's where you will feel whether you're interested in a person then use your head because you'll need it to figure out if the relationship is sustainable. I have to say that you haven't been using your head. I was once a young man who made mistakes. As a grown man and as a husband, I've made a lot. Some of which I'm not proud of and if you ask me, that young man has made the biggest mistake. I hope he learns from it. What I also hope is, you, my daughter, realize that life is love, hurt, pain, joy, and happiness. Sometimes we experience all of it in one day. Mistakes happen in life.

Learn from this. This too shall pass, and know that you are tough and strong. I want you to know that I love you. One thing I know for sure is that I don't have to worry about you. You can take care of yourself. I know you can. Why? You have that Braham blood inside of ya. You'll be fine. So, wake up girl and shake it off. You'll be fine."

As a daddy's girl, I hung onto every little word he said to me and never forgot it. Have you ever looked up to someone so much that it didn't matter what they said to you? You will always have their wisdom embedded in your heart. That was what it was like for me whenever my father spoke. My eager eyes would watch him slowly speak as he chose his words methodically. He had a way of spewing wise words into you without you feeling bad about yourself. I felt so much better after he gave me that talk. I didn't even say a word. All I did was drink my hot cup of tea and my Shirley Biscuits while fighting back the tears.

My tears didn't last long because February of 2005, I graduated from Brooklyn College. All the required classes with the necessary credits to graduate were completed. I was going to walk down the campus aisle with my dad by my side. It was one of the proudest moments of his life and mine.

To be the first generation in my family to graduate college meant a great deal to my parents. To see my father's face lit up as I walked by his row with him holding the video camera, his other camera dangled around his neck from its straps, his sunglasses perched up on his nose while wearing a huge smile. It was a beautiful sight to behold. He later joked that he forgot how not to smile that day because his face was hurting him so much from smiling the entire day. He was so happy! My father was right.

Life is hurt

Life is pain

Life is Joy

Life is Happiness

The happiness I felt the day I graduated outweighed the hurt I felt leading up to it. It was now time to proudly embark on my journey to the unknown. Wherever that would lead me, I knew for sure my father was going to be right there by my side.

THE HAPPY WITHIN YOU CHALLENGE

Write down a time when everything in your life was going great and suddenly an unannounced challenge or life changing event happened. Name three things/ people/tools or experiences that helped you heal through the process.

.... 4 ....
THE PATRIARCHAL TRUTH

"To change radically, does not mean to do something drastic, it
means to do something rooted in logic, and there's nothing more
rooted in logic than a mind replacing misconceptions with truths."

-Minna Salami, Author

Here's the truth. Some black men are not living up to
their parental obligations. However, it is completely
abhorrent for societies to view black fathers as non-
capable, uncaring or as deadbeat fathers. A black man steps out
into the world and immediately the public's opinion of him goes
up. Some might be positive, but a lot of it is, unfortunately, a
one-dimensional perception. He's not a good father. He doesn't
take care of his children. He doesn't want to get a job. He's not
spending time with his children. There is no magic formula to
becoming a perfect father because there is no such thing as a
perfect father. However, there are many great black fathers using
the best tools possible to provide, protect and create the best life
for their children.

There is a world where black patriarchy exists in the form of creating
stability and structure within the household or family dynamic.

There are black single fathers taking care of their children. There
are stay at home fathers changing diapers. There are black fathers who
are co-parenting with the mothers of their children and doing it with
greatness and zeal! There are black father's whose dominant authority
helps to create strong foundations within their household and they

make critical thinking decisions for their families. This is positive, not negative. Personally, I have not seen many of those positive stories being told. However, do not be absorbent at the notion that black fathers are absent. Black fathers are still powerful in their paternal roles because:

- **They set the example as the role model for their children - They take pride in taking care of their children.**

- **They value the relationship they have with their children.**

- **They impart a sense of influence that enhances their children's identity.**

When I think about my own father, I think about our living room conversations. I think about our backyard conversations, sitting on the stoop laughing and learning. I think about when I was a little girl how he would light up when I came home from school. I think about him helping me with my homework especially when it was related to history and political science. Those were his favorite topics. I dared not debate him on those because he would always win anyway. Even throughout my adulthood, he never failed to ask me how my day was. When I think about those special moments, it makes me appreciate the fact that my father was interested in knowing about me. He valued my attention as much as I valued his. He was making sure that I was alright, by doing so, helping to cultivate my inner confidence I didn't know I had. When I matured into a woman, he was still fathering me. He was still spending time with me. He was still sharing his intellectual wisdom. If my father had not partaken in the molding and shaping of my upbringing, I'm not sure I would have been able to be comfortable communicating to anyone from anywhere unafraid!

Most fathers' routines involve getting up to go to work to earn a decent living. Midnight shifts, early morning commutes, whether working as a hard laborer in jeans and a hard hat or working in an office space in a nice button-down shirt and tie, they are focused on getting to work to provide. It saddens me, however, to have witnessed on few occasions black fathers commuting to work or just going about their daily lives being judged by others without them even saying a word.

I once witnessed a man getting on the train early in the morning. It might have been 5am. He had his coffee in one hand and a bagel in the other. As he entered the train, I saw him searching around looking for somewhere to sit. He spotted a seat in the middle of the aisle, so he walked toward it carefully as to not spill the coffee or drop his bagel since the train was wobbling side to side. I remember just watching him because not only was he a very tall man, probably 6'6, but he had a distinctive walk due to him being bowed-legged. He was casually dressed, clean cut, wearing his man bag crossway over his shoulder. He seemed to be middle-age, maybe in his 50's. He approached the seat and gestured to a lady, who was taking up part of the seat that he wanted to sit there. She looked up at him and hesitated but then slowly slides to the other side of the ceramic seat giving him just enough room for him to sit. He paired up the coffee and the bagel in one hand, so he could use the other one to hold unto to the railing as a balance for him to sit in precision. I was impressed by his skill and I remember chuckling a little.

Sitting comfortably now, and ready to finish his breakfast, the lady next to him screamed out, "Don't touch my bag!" She screamed so loud everyone in that car, quickly looked in their direction. The man looked puzzled, but quickly ignored her and carried on eating his bagel. Moments later, she once again screamed, "Don't touch my bag!" This time she stood up. The man, now very annoyed, defended himself by telling her that he was not touching her bag. A fellow passenger sitting across from them shouted to the lady, "Ma'am, stop it. That man did not touch your bag." Refusing to accept that, she began to spew all sorts of words at the man, yelling and wailing even suggesting for him to find another seat.

Realizing the man was not budging, she addressed the rest of the passengers on the train and shouted, "You see how these people are?" Pointing towards the man. They're always trying to take what's not theirs. I don't know why he chose to sit next to me anyway. You stupid imbecile!"

This lady was a short, Caucasian woman who was very irate and insulting. I wasn't too sure whether to describe her as deranged because clearly, she was speaking in complete sentences. To me, she knew exactly what she was saying and doing, creating an unnecessary scene. At this point, we all could see the man getting extremely upset. I remember saying to myself, "Please, just relax. Stay calm." hoping he would hear my inner thoughts, so he wouldn't make the wrong move. As quickly as I had that thought, he stood up facing the woman and furiously said, "I am going to pray for you lady. I know what your problem is, you didn't want this black man to sit next to you, uh? So, you made up this lie!" Now, this was getting interesting. There were a few passengers playing peacemakers. Some were pretending to ignore the situation, but others were encouraging him to stand up and defend himself.

One man even shouted. "Yes, it's true my brother. It's true you're talking." I felt so bad for the man, however, as he continued to speak, what he said next made my eyes fill up with tears. Bowlegged, 6'6 in height and all, he stood there, and he screamed as loud as he could with almost a crackle in his voice, "People like me lady are hard - working! I'm sick and tired of this, man! I'm sick and tired of people like you judging me because I'm black, because that's what it is. I'm just trying to make it to work lady!" He went on: "I have five kids I gotta take care of. Five!" I get up early every morning. I take this same train every morning to go to work, so I can take care of them and I gotta deal with people like YOU! All I want to do is go to work and make it back home to my kids in one-piece lady." He walked over to the opposite side where some other guy gestured for him to sit by him.

It was a moment I would never forget because I could hear the hurt and frustration in his voice. I could see that this experience was nothing new to him. It was a day he decided he had enough, and he wasn't going to take it anymore. For me, the moment he said, "I just want to make it home to my kids" was the moment he realized what was important. The altercation could have played out into something worse. He could have reacted differently, and the police might have been involved. The lady could have pulled the emergency brakes and stopped the train causing a delay. The passengers would have had to wait who knows how long for the police to show up. He could have ended up in jail that morning because of a lie that was told on him. All of that did not happen because he thought about his children. The first thing that came to his mind were his children. They were important.

One of the greatest decisions a father must make is deciding what it is he will do to create a positive impact for his children. It's no different for a black father who wants the same things as any other father, without the limitation society places on them or the false stereotypical rhetoric which can negatively influence their daily lives, and perhaps affect how they raise their children.

When I was mind-mapping the idea about writing this book in the summer of 2015, I knew I wanted to share some of my experiences I had with my father and the impact he made on my life, but I also wanted to include other fathers and daughters who had similar bonds to be a part of it. I wanted to learn from them. These fathers come from different cultural backgrounds, have different beliefs, but share one thing in common, and that is the love they have for their daughters. That love is simply immeasurable. I can unapologetically say that I am the beneficiary of that said immeasurable love from my own father. It's time society celebrate these fathers and acknowledge their contribution to their children's lives.

According to a C.D.C report[6], It was concluded that black fathers were just as involved in their children's lives in comparison to their counterparts. Spending quality time and participating in every stage of a daughter's life will help boost her confidence and allow her to be aware of her self-identity.

As mentioned before, I needed to explore ways in how I could change society's perception that black fathers are not there for their children, at the same time heighten the awareness of the positive impact fathers have on their daughters. I know, first- hand, if it wasn't for my father's constant love and attention, I would not have graduated college. I would not have the confidence that I have about myself and knowing who I am, where I come from, and being proud of all of that. Also, just so you know, fathers can learn a lot from their daughters as much as they can from their sons. In the proceeding pages, you will be introduced to three amazing fathers and four daughters sharing what they have learned from each other and offering a bit of advice.

2006–2010'. December 2013

You will read about the love they have for each other but also challenges they faced as a father, as a daughter, and how they overcame those challenges. In the end, because of their father-daughter love and experiences, they are who they are today. These fathers lived up to their parental obligations even during times of doubt and disappointments. You'll also meet Bintou, a daughter who although was raised in a strict household, hung on to the very word of her father's mantra, "Be content with what you have." His spiritual love for her gave her the stability and ability to persevere.

[6] Jones. Jo, Ph.D., and Mosher. William D., Ph.D., Division of Vital Statistics. 'Fathers' Involvement With Their Children: United States,

~ANSELMO MIGUEL ESTWICK~

"My everyday life experience as a young dad was good based on guidance that I was given growing

up, the positive things that I was told of life's expectations...to always do my best in my daily efforts."

Meet Anselmo, born in the Republic of Panama in 1951. He's described by his daughter, Cassandra, as an old school Panamanian who's very expressive and enjoys a good conversation. Anselmo, like my dad, were from a different generation of fathers. They valued education and prided themselves on having a strong work ethic with strict convictions. Just 27 years old when Cassandra was born, Mr. Anselmo knew he had to provide for his family by any means necessary. As he mentions in his interview, he was "ecstatically happy" when Cassandra was born and today the bond between them is "a great one."

How prepared were you when Cassandra was born?

I was very prepared to be a father to Cassandra

How was the relationship between you and your father?

My father and I had a very good relationship.

Growing up, who were your father figures/role models?

Growing up, my biggest male father figure and role model was my grandfather. My father was in the United States, so I looked up to my grandfather.

What kind of work were you doing when Cassandra was born?

I was a salesman at a stationary store.

Could you discuss a little bit about some of the challenges you faced trying to raise your family?

At that time, I was not earning enough money to send them to a private school or buy a house. I had applied for a job as a bookkeeper but was told that my handwriting was not great so they offered me the salesman job earning 1/3 of what the bookkeeper job paid, but I took it in order to provide for my family without asking for handouts from anyone or the government. It was hard, but I managed to provide food on the table, clothing on their backs, medical coverage, and a roof over our heads.

Share a poignant story about your experiences being a young dad. What affect if any, do you think it had on your daughter?

My everyday life experience as a young dad was good based on my guidance that I was given growing up, and positive things that I was told of life's expectations. I was told to always do my best in my daily efforts. I never mixed work with my home life. I worked hard in order to raise and provide the necessary things for my 4 daughters, wife and assist my mother also. I believe that this made them all to be very strong and to respect themselves.

How different was it to raise your daughter compared to raising her siblings?

It was no different raising Cassandra than the way I raised her other sisters. I taught them to be strong, respectful, and ambitious women. I had 4 beautiful daughters, no son, but I would not have said anything different to a son.

What is the fondest memory you have of Cassandra?

My fondest memory that I have of Cassandra is that she graduated from high school at the age of 16, and got her associate's degree at the age of 18 with high grades.

What are some of the goals that you want from your daughter currently?

At this time, I do not need anything from Cassandra only that she stays healthy and happy.

Give an example of a time when you felt that your daughter let you down. What happened, and how did you deal with that situation?

At no given time or occasion did I feel or ever felt that Cassandra let me down I have always been very proud of her and the goals that she has accomplished.

When you hear the word responsible fathering, what does that mean to you?

When I hear the word responsible fathering, that means to me a person who takes the responsibility in providing for their family, being there for them and taking charge. Nurturing them. Giving them stability. Not making excuses as to what you can and can't do for them.

What advice do you have for young fathers today who might not be sure about being a father or who may not have the tools about being there for their children?

The advice that I have for the young fathers of today is to be a man. Work hard and be a father to their children. Show them love and bring them up in a good environment so that they can be a better person in society. Don't give up because these kids did not ask to be here.

What would you like to be your legacy for your daughter?

My legacy for my daughters would be that they would be financially set for the future based on the property, savings, insurance, and jewelries to be shared among them.

Was there a time where you felt you made a mistake with your Cassandra? How did you feel about that?

It was not being able to send them to private school for a better education.

What do you see in your daughter that she may not see in herself?

The same things I see in my daughter is the same things that she sees in herself. She is ambitious in reaching her goals. The sky is the limit.

What have you learned about life that you wished you learned at your daughter's age?

I should have been preparing more financially for the future.

~CASSANDRA ESTWICK~

"Start a conversation with your dad about your feelings. If you find it hard to talk to your dad, try

writing a letter, but you must let him know how you feel so you both can work on healing the relationship."

The gift of life! Cassandra Estwick knows exactly how it feels to receive a father's love more than we'll ever know. Cassandra, an entrepreneur was born in Brooklyn, New York and was raised by her Panamanian father Angelsmo. She was very enthusiastic to be a part of this book and to share her story. Her close relationship with her dad is as transparent and loving as ever.

How is your relationship with your father today?

I am very close with my dad. Although I don't get to hang out with him as much as we used to because I moved across the country, we still text, video chat and talk often.

What is the best memory that you have of your father?

I don't know if this is necessarily the best memory, but it is one of the better memories I have for sure. My dad is very much into celebrating in general and he always made sure all holidays were special. I remember one particular year during the winter, I was probably about 9 years old at the time. We had an incident where my parents had a safe stolen from our home. I didn't know the safe existed until this day when my dad was understandably furious. He was talking to my mom about the missing safe. I recall he was very upset about it and I overheard him telling my mom something about everything being gone.

This incident happened probably 2 weeks before Christmas, and I remember that on Christmas morning instead of the plethora of toys we would normally have, my sisters and I each had one box under our Christmas tree. We each had a dress inside of the box, nothing fancy at all but they were dresses. That morning during our breakfast and after opening our gifts my dad tried his best to explain that he wanted to get us toys especially because we did so well in school, but he wasn't able to because of the safe being stolen.

We assured him that we understood but we could all tell that he felt guilty about not being able to make this Christmas as spectacular as he normally does. That day, after breakfast, my sisters and I all got dressed wearing the dresses that my dad got us, and we surprised him. I remember that he cried and told us how sweet that was, and we went on our day playing music and enjoying each other.

How would you describe your dad growing up?

My dad is from Panama with Jamaican grandparents, so he has Caribbean customs. Growing up he was a typical parent from the Caribbean—he was very strict when it came to school, chores and of course boys! What I can say is that he has always worked very hard and been a great provider for the family. He was also the parent who was always ready to party and listen to music. He had no filter when talking to us about the realities of being a black girl/woman in the world, and he spoke to us in the realest way which we always appreciated.

Did your father ever speak to you about how you should choose a partner?

Absolutely. He always told us not to deal with anyone who is lesser than we are. For example, if you are working, make sure your partner is working the same or harder than you. He gave us points on how your partner should treat you. How they should make you happy, because you can do bad all by yourself.

Growing up did you feel like you could go to your father for advice rather than you would your mother? If so, talk about some of those advice.

I was equally close with both of my parents and honestly, I felt comfortable talking to either of them about advice. Some of the advice I spoke with my dad about was definitely school related.

Anytime I came across tough issues. I also certainly got advice from him about how to take care of myself and stand up for myself.

What were some expectations you had, as you researched how your father grew up? How have those expectations influenced your decision making in what you look for in a committed partner?

Well because of the person my dad was I always expected him to be home (except when he was in Panama). I expected him to work and provide for all of us. I expected him to fix things around the house. I expected him to help with everything really. My dad is very intelligent and speaks 3 languages. He has always been an avid learner, so I basically felt that anything I had a question about, I expected him to know the answer or get the answer. These expectations influenced me when I started dating and eventually married my husband because I look for these same qualities in my partner.

Give me an example where your father disappointed you, realized it and later apologized. How did that disappointment make you feel?

Listen, no one is perfect. I have had times that I believe I was disappointed by my father for sure. Whether it was how he handled a family dispute or how he disciplined me, the disappointment didn't feel good. I can remember feeling hurt or saddened by my dad, absolutely. I cannot think of a specific incident where he did something and then apologized for it. He was not an apologetic person growing up at all, but I do know that when I was grown up and moved out of the house he did apologize for as he said, "being too hard on me" as a child but wanted to let me know that it was because he wanted to keep me protected.

How would you describe the relationship with your father now?

I believe we have a typical close relationship now. I can call my dad for anything. He still sends me gifts, money, etc. just as when I was a child living at home. He is close with my daughter and husband as well, and it is pretty much the same as when I was growing up.

What has been the most valuable life lessons that your father has taught you?

Not to get taken advantage of and to have pride in myself. Also, the importance of having family around and taking care of one another. He is very big on family and I am the same way.

Do you feel that your father has influenced you as to how you choose a partner or make decisions within a romantic relationship? How?

Yes, certainly because I saw how growing up my dad was always around and how he always did things for my mom like buying her flowers and taking care of her. My mom was a stay at home mom because that is what she and my dad decided and although I wanted a career, I still wanted a partner that treated me the way I saw my dad treated my mom.

Give me an example of a time when your father was very supportive of you even when he knew you were not making the right decision.

Probably when I was with my ex- boyfriend. My dad saw what my young eyes did not see at the time. Even though he knew this was not a good person for me he supported my decision to be with that person and made every effort to include him in our family.

What are some of the qualities your father have that you would like to have in a partner?

Intellectual, hardworking, generous, and fun.

What advice do you have for daughters who may feel like their relationship with their dad isn't the way they would like for it to be?

I would say to start the conversation with your dad about your feelings. If you find it hard to talk to your dad, try writing a letter but you must let him know how you feel so you both can work on healing the relationship.

What do you see in your father that he may not see in himself?

That he is extremely smart and great at a multitude of things. He is just used to being the problem solver for the family without realizing how intelligent he is.

What was that one mistake dad made and you forgave him for it unconditionally?

Probably not moving when we had the opportunity. I realized years later that he decided we would not move because my mother wanted to stay close to her siblings.

Explain why it's so important for a father to be involved in their children's life, particularly their daughter's life?

Well your father is essentially the first male that you will have in your life and that relationship will most certainly dictate how you perceive men should be in your life. Whether you want a man who is similar or NOT similar, it will be influenced by your father in my opinion. I know countless women who did not have their dad in their lives growing up, and I personally see the difference in how their relationships with guys were growing up. So many of them were sexually active and pregnant way before I was even thinking of those activities. So many of them have children with multiple men because they unfortunately are looking for love in the wrong places in my opinion. I know this is not always the case but, in my life, it has proven to be the case for many women that I know.

If you had one word to describe your father what word would that be?

GENEROUS. When I was only 19 years old, I was diagnosed with a debilitating kidney disease. It hit me like a ton of bricks because I was always a very health conscious person and athlete. My family took the news as hard as me and they all comforted me during the darkest of times. Without hesitation, my father gave me one of his kidneys. He never told anyone. He just did it. He came to every dialysis treatment, every doctor's appointment. He paid $1000 for a single medication that I needed post-transplant because my employer fired me when I came back from medical leave and

I didn't have insurance temporarily—my dad came to my rescue. He has done so many generous things not only for me but for almost everyone in my entire family and strangers. That is why we love him so much.

RELEASE YOUR VULNERABILITIES AND EXPRESS YOURSELF

My short-lived relationship with Terrence taught me a lot about myself. It taught me not to be so gullible in love. It taught me how to listen to my gut, but I must admit, I was vulnerable after the break up. I did not want to expose myself in fear of being hurt again. I didn't want to feel inadequate. I could hear my father's earnest voice saying, "Be tough. Stay strong. You can take care of yourself." His faith in me allowed me to grow an extra layer of thick skin which perhaps numbed all feelings inside of ever being in a relationship anytime soon.

Being vulnerable does not come easy for me. I don't think it comes easy for a lot of people. As women, we're often subjected to phrases like:

"You're strong."

" Be a strong, black woman."

We think we must continue to portray this superhero strength; be the woman who can handle everything. I suppose we can tackle many challenges, but some of those challenges come with its burdens and can take a toll on us emotionally, leaving us feeling powerless. Not showing any form of weakness is a false pretense. As I've gotten older, I had to learn that for me to grow and begin to trust again, I had to be open. I had to be able to release my vulnerabilities and express myself. Express how you are feeling. Express how you are not feeling. If there is something you feel like doing, do it. Even if you doubt yourself.

One of my very first acts of expressing how I truly felt about a situation happened in 1994. It was my father who convinced me to express my thoughts and my feelings. Dad taught me to not only express myself, but to commit to always putting my best foot forward. There was this one time in April of 1994 where my father and I were watching the evening news. We witnessed a historic event. A world-renowned hero, a brave man, would be running for president. Millions of black people for the first time ever would vote for him.

He would later become the president of a country that had imprisoned him for 27 years. This event was such a poignant moment for the world. I knew how this moment affected me in such a positive way, and I wondered at the time if others in my class felt the same way. As we discussed the making of history, my father encouraged me to write about it and share my thoughts on this historic moment with my teacher and classmates. I was hesitant at first. I did not want to do it, but after a long conversation about it with my father, I thought it would be a great idea. I became excited and couldn't wait to share my speech with my classmates.

I was fourteen years old at the time attending a catholic school in the Bushwick area of Brooklyn, New York. The nuns were strict and walked around with very unpleasant expressions on their faces at times. I spoke to one of the nuns about my idea and she thought it was so brave of me wanting to do that. She told me to write what I wanted to say, and afterwards graciously complimented my father, stating how special it was to have an amazing father like I do.

I truly felt great that my father was the one who sparked the idea. I went home after school and started writing. I read the short essay out loud to my father, and he proudly approved, giving me the thumbs up. The next day, I enthusiastically, showed the short speech to the nun. She glanced at it but didn't budge. Her look and her demeanor suggested that she wasn't inclined for me to present the speech to the class. The zealous deposition she had the day before was not the same. She seemed almost surprised that I actually wrote the speech.

I ended up waiting until the end of the class to ask her if I was going to read the speech. She told me it was too late but assured me first thing tomorrow she would allow me to recite it. I was a little disappointed, however I was looking forward to the morning.

The next day, in front of the class, she praised me again for taking the initiative to write such a speech. She stood in the middle of the classroom, held my speech close to her face, and began to read it out loud. I was a bit bewildered. I felt proud because she was reading my speech, but I thought I was going to read my own speech. The students applauded and cheered me on as she returned my speech. She stood there clapping with a subtle smile on her face and grinningly said, "Nice job." I was very upset that I didn't get to recite my speech. I went home and shared what happened with my father. He was pleased that my speech was read. However, he was not too keen it was the nun who read my speech and not me. I expressed to him how I wished the entire school heard my speech.

The following morning, my father went to work late because what he was planning on doing that morning was very important to him. Usually, my father doesn't accompany me to school, but on this morning, he did. I had no idea what he was going to do, but I knew my father had a temper when it came to his children being wronged by someone. No one messes with his children! I remember asking him what he was going to do. He simply answered, "Don't you worry about that." I was extremely nervous not for myself but for whomever he was going to butt heads with. He felt it was necessary without a question to demonstrate the magnitude of this historical event in an effective way.

My speech would be heard on a larger scale this time. My hand in his hand, he walked me into the principal's office. Now, right before you get to the principal's office, you had to get to the receptionist desk. He saw Ms. Nolan, the secretary of the school, a very tall dark-skinned woman with a noticeable pointed nose. Her glasses were always worn on the tip of her nose, almost touching her painted red lips. She was always happy to see my father because of the shared cultural similarities. My father and her would have various conversations from time to time about the Panamanians and the Jamaicans. I remember on one occasion when my father went to pay my school fee, they talked about the collaboration between the Panamanians and the Jamaicans building the Panama Canal. So naturally, my father felt comfortable speaking with her and vice versa.

In a soft- spoken tone, my father turned to her and said, "You know Ms. Nolan, my daughter wrote a little speech and she didn't get the opportunity to read it, so I would like for her to share that speech on the loud speaker, so the entire school could hear how important this moment has changed the world. If you could just give her 3 minutes, that would be great." Miss Nolan said, "Not a problem, but she would have to ask Sister Mary, the Principal."

My father at first didn't want her to ask the principal because he pointed out that the intercom was right in our eyesight and reading the speech wouldn't take long, but Ms. Nolan insisted on asking Sister Mary. I thought Sister Mary would deny us, but once my father explained to her why he believes the entire school should hear the speech, she agreed. We waited until all the children were settled into their classrooms. The bell rang as all the children were slowing piling in. I glanced over at my father, and the look on his face was priceless, he had a smirking smile. I knew in his mind he was saying to himself, "Got em!" He took the paper out of his coat pocket and handed it to me and quietly said, "Say your name and which class you're from. Then introduce what you're about to say." I remember Sister Mary walked up closely beside me. She held down the lever on the intercom to ensure everyone would hear me. I said my name, which class I belonged to, then read the speech in an almost gravitas tone. I was nervous, but It was the most gratifying experience. With a high five, a hug and a kiss on the cheek my father said, "That's my girl. See you later." as he walked out and headed off to work. I received so much praise from Ms. Nolan and Sister Mary. When I walked into my home room class everyone clapped and cheered me on. It was a warm, emotional feeling I felt that day. I was so happy and proud of myself.

"On this day April 27th, 1994, let us celebrate and acknowledge this historic achievement not just for the people of South Africa, but for all black Africans and all people around the world. For the first time in its history, millions of black South Africans will be casting their votes in its very first election ending the nations' apartheid era and bringing in the new with hope and prosperity. Let us celebrate the accomplishments and sacrifices of the African National Congress presidential candidate, Nelson Mandela, a man who after 27 years of imprisonment will be casting his vote for the first time, seeking to become the first Black African President of South Africa. Let us all say Uhura! Uhura!"

-Allison Braham, recited at Saint Elizabeth Seton School,

Brooklyn, NY

I didn't fully understand at the time why my father took it upon himself to escort me to school, so I could recite the speech, but looking back, what he was doing was helping me build my confidence. He was allowing me to express myself freely and at the same time encouraging me to take a stance in something I believed in. I've now come to understand that to build confidence is an essential part of a child's growth and development, and it is a father's responsibility to aide in that effort. My father helped me to build my confidence, and he provided me with a good foundation where I was able to be myself.

If you are a father reading this book, you have the power to help build your child's confidence especially your daughters' confidence. Daughter's take more chances when their fathers are engaged with them, and by doing so, they're not afraid to express themselves when they are

- **Feeling hurt**

- **Afraid or unsure about something**

- **Wanting to speak up about something they care deeply about**

Naming a Teddy Bear?

Even during times of challenges, it's important to push through and release your vulnerabilities. I remember when my father was sick and, in the hospital, a friend of mine brought him a teddy bear. and My friend asked him, "What are you going to name the teddy bear?" I remember he looked at us with a peculiar reaction as if to say, "Give a speechless, emotionless object a name?" He thought that was silly but after a little coercing, he looked at the teddy bear and thought about it for a second then said, "Rambo." I thought that was quite significant.

Rambo for him represented strength, a fighter who does not back down. He wanted to show strength and stamina even in his vulnerable state. He wanted us to know subliminally that he's strong, he's a fighter, and Teddy Rambo (as our family now calls the teddy bear), was a representation of that strength. Being vulnerable is a beautiful thing because it demonstrates your humanness. There is nothing more human than to express how you truly feel emotionally. We all have experienced a time when we weren't feeling our best emotionally. When we have those feelings, it's so easy to suppress them in fear that once we expose those feelings we may be judged or perhaps others may use your vulnerabilities against you. I've had those experiences and therefore as a result, I would shut down.

As I've gotten older, I have learned that it is okay to release your vulnerabilities and express how you feel. If you feel that someone is going to judge you it is not your issue it is their issue. They either can help you or not help you. You must express yourself because you don't know who can help you and can relate to what you are going through.

There is this limiting belief that sharing our scared inhibitions will only bring about shame and judgement, and we may feel like others will not understand what you are going through. That is quite the contrary. Releasing your vulnerable emotions only helps make you stronger. Your story may very well inspire someone to change their lives. At every stage of my life so far, I have embraced my vulnerabilities, and have become better at expressing how I feel. Suppressing your emotions to prove you are strong only suffocates the person you are truly meant to be.

"It Appears that Vulnerability is also the birthplace of joy and creativity, of belonging, and of love."

-Brene Brown

When I decided to write this book, I knew exactly what it would be about. It would be about my father and the father/daughter relationship we had together. What is so interesting is it took losing my father for me to decide on writing a book. In the process of doing so, I questioned myself many times. I asked myself:

- **Can I really write this book?**

- **Will I be judged?**

- **Will people find value in the book?**

- **Will people buy the book?**

- **Will I be satisfied with the outcome of the book?**

At one point I stopped writing because I was still emotionally vulnerable. My thoughts were muddled in the idea of people reading something that was so special and dear to my heart. I thought about what they would say, what they will not say. I admit, I was slightly timid, but I came to understand later that the fear of the unknown was what created that vulnerable side in me and I wanted it to stop. The truth is, to stop feeling vulnerable is unrealistic, especially when you desire something great for your life. Vulnerability is necessary and releasing your vulnerabilities is liberating. There is not one influential leader or writer who have not experienced a time in their lives when they did not feel vulnerable. They are many successful leaders who speak to thousands of people all over the world and I'm sure they have had similar questions and doubts, but they survived it. They embraced their vulnerabilities while sharing their gifts to the world, and in doing so freed themselves in the process.

Here's my confession: there have been times when I cried while writing this book. I laughed. I jumped up for joy. I became frustrated as I stared at the blank computer screen not knowing what to write, then after four hours, filled the blank page with only a paragraph, in which I perhaps edited three or more times. When these emotions creep up inside of me, I get motivated even more to continue. I accepted being vulnerable while writing the book because I know its apart of the process. Ultimately, my desire is to share the love I had with my father and share the stories of other daughters and fathers who have that same love. If one or two people are inspired by this book, that will not be a failure, that will be a success.

"Vulnerability is being willing to express the truth no matter what. The Truth of who you are; the essence at your core, of what you're feeling at any given moment. It's being able to open up your soul and let it flow so that other people can see their souls in yours."

– Oprah Winfrey

THE HAPPY WITHIN YOU CHALLENGE

Write down two examples of a time where your father helped to build up your confidence when you were vulnerable or unwilling to express yourself?

.... 6 ....
SELF- CONFIDENCE WITHIN THE BLACK DAUGHTER

I wasn't always confident growing up. Although my parents instilled traditional values that were aligned with how they were brought up to help my self-esteem, I still had to face challenges outside of the home. I was so thankful to have an amazing father to guide me along the way when those challenges arose. Dad was always there as a resource; sharing his wisdom and letting me know about my self-worth. After graduating college, it was time to look for the job of my dreams, and I couldn't wait to get out into the trenches and start the process. Jones, New York, Tahari and Lands' End business suits were the go-to brands I needed to wear for those interviews. Macy's here I come! The thought of working in media excited me; it gave me immediate thrill just thinking about the people I'd meet and the connections I'd make.

I remember the morning of my first big interview with one of the major news stations in New York. I had butterflies in my stomach so badly I thought I would end up being late because I kept going to the bathroom. That's how nervous I was. The night before I studied the top 10 interview questions and answers for a Media/Production Assistant. I pretended I was the interviewer and interviewee while looking in the mirror. My father pretended to be the hiring manager. He put on this black suit with a white button-down shirt and sat in the living room with no shoes on his feet, just the suit and the shirt. I looked at him and said, "Dad If you were the hiring manger, I would ask to speak to your manager and ask why they allowed a bare footed, ugly toe man with wrangled suit work here." We both burst out in laughter.

The practice session really helped, and as I walked to the train station, I replayed every question and answer I practiced with my dad. I even had a cheat sheet with the questions I was reading. I was prepared. When I got off 59Th street, I took in a deep breath. The 4-block walk to the building seemed like forever and a day. What you must know is New Yorkers are accustomed to walking long blocks. It's not a problem for us. What becomes a problem is walking those long blocks in high heels plus having to make sure your hair stays in place as the whirling wind gushes and swoops it back and forth.

When I arrived, I was greeted by the receptionist who handed me the paper application to fill out. When I sat down, I looked around to see if there were other interviewees, and there were three other women waiting. The competition looked stiff, but I was ready. I was the second person to be called. The interviewer came out, she called my name while walking over to the other lady who was sitting directly across from the receptionist. "Allison Braham?" She extended her hand to the other girl, assuming that she was me. The girl shakes her head, no. I then raised my hand and said, "I'm Allison Braham." The reaction she gave me was a look of surprise as she looked down unto her legal pad. I guess it was to look at my name once more to make sure she wasn't making a mistake. In that moment, I owned up to the fact that not only does my name has power but made me think about how others viewed me based on my name before even meeting me.

There was a subtle bias towards my name which did not match up to how I looked. She immediately pictured the other girl as Allison Braham and most likely gave me another name. I felt confused in that moment and thought, "I'm I not going to get this job because of how I look?" How I look doesn't match up to my name and that's not what they were looking for.

I went into the board room and was greeted by four other producers and writers. My stomach started rattling. I made sure I looked each of them in the eye and introduced myself with a not so friendly, but assertive tone. I sat down, and my knees began to shake. What seemed to be a five-minute silence was just that, silent eyes, lots of eyes staring at me. "Why are you here?" the executive producer asked while her head was positioned down towards my resume. I couldn't tell if she had a crooked hunch back neck or she was just mesmerized by my resume.

"I am here for the Associate Producer's position," I answered with a slight tremble in my voice. She stared at me once again and asked, "Yeah, we get that, but why are you here?" I was confused. I asked her if she could be more specific with her question and she boldly replied, "No." I quickly rethought in that moment to flip it. I was already nervous, and the feeling of anger was slowly creeping inside. "I am here for the same reason that you are. You're here to see if I'm the right fit for this position as AP, and I'm here to see if you and this organization is the right fit for me to work for. That got her attention. All eyes on me, this time with their heads moving around looking at each other.

I didn't feel right in my body about this interview. It felt more like an interrogation. I practiced all these questions and answers and here comes 'Miserable Mandy' throwing me off for the loop. When I told my father how I answered her, he laughed so hard and championed me for standing up and being firm. The entire interview lasted 20 minutes and it appeared to me that 'Miserable Mandy' intimidated the other producers. After all, she was the only one asking the questions. I truly could not understand why, but I was determined to go through the process, and I was not going to be intimidated.

After a 20-minute interrogation, I walked out of the room feeling depleted but proud of myself because I did it. I endured questions like:

"Where are you from? You don't sound like you're from Brooklyn."

"Are you comfortable being surrounded by high profile men?" What does 'not sounding like you're from Brooklyn' have to do with getting the job?

I went home crying, wondering if this was the industry I truly wanted to be a part of. I felt slightly judged in that interview. I didn't understand why they were acting in that manner. But I also felt like my name didn't match up to their image of how I looked. That was a problem. My name was right for the job, but maybe the color of my skin was not. I had all these questions. I was the only black candidate who applied for that position, so that was my initial thought.

That experience made me feel so vulnerable. I remember going straight into the living room replaying the questions that were asked, and I just sat on the couch staring into space thinking I'm not going to get the job. My father came into the living room very excited but saw my not so exhilarated demeanor. He knew something was wrong. He sat next to me and asked, "What's wrong with my angel?" I shared with him what happened.

"They were so cold dad, so cold." I turned to him. I still could not believe what I experienced on my first real interview. My father's initial response was not what I expected, but being a caring dad, he turned to me and said, "It was probably just all an act to see how you would respond to them. They were trying to intimidate you, that's all. I think they were blown away by your beauty and brains, because as far as I'm concerned, the way you answered those questions was nothing but sheer intelligence and class. You're gonna get that job!" He pumped his fist in the air.

I wasn't too sure if they were impressed by me, but I couldn't help but to curl up on the couch, still in my interview suit, smelling the newness of it, and the tag I forgot to remove before due to my nervousness. I looked quite professional however, and I was proud to have purchased that Tahari suit.

I lingered in the living room for about an hour that morning watching television. I decided it was time to get over my sulking. I eventually lugged along into the kitchen for something to eat. After fixing myself a sandwich, I walked over to the table to sit down. I saw there was a piece of napkin on top of the table with a beautiful sunflower. On the napkin was a simple note that read:

"I'M PROUD OF YOU. LOVE, DAD"

In caps and all, as dad would often write in, I stared at the note, and a huge smile brushed my lips. I remember feeling so happy, and in that moment all that sulking and puffing withered away in an instant. That act of love was my father's signature style, writing notes around the house whether it was to say, "I love you." or "Don't forget to take the meat out the freezer so it can thaw". He would leave notes not just for me but for my brothers and mother too. Whatever the note was, his complimentary close was always, "Love, Dad."

My father loved writing. He would get great pleasure putting pen to paper. He had his own unique style of writing. For me his writings were beautiful works of art. I suppose this is where I get that passion for it, it's in my DNA. I once asked him when I was putting together his book of poems, "Why do you enjoy writing poems so much? And who inspired you?" He answered, "It's about putting words together to make sense, like Geneopous to Termiopous (a poem he wrote while living in England about love and marriage.) I really, really enjoyed writing that poem. Although it took me a long time. It was a hard task putting words together for that poem. And yet it became the most difficult poem I've ever attempted to do. My less difficult one was Mountain Mary, that took me 20 minutes. As for inspiration, music gives me inspiration." (Excerpt from, Memoirs in Poetry 2013)

My father was definitely my inspiration and I knew that whatever the decision was regarding my interview, I would have my father in my corner rooting for me and I would be able to lean on him for counsel.

His mere presence just being there and listening to me; giving me a word of advice was important for me. I believed also, that he believed by doing such was his patriarchal duty. I also believe it gave him pure joy to be my sounding board.

The phone rang and I noticed a 212-area code which looked familiar, so I immediately took in a deep breath as this might be "The CALL" as to whether or not I got the job. I answered in a very firm but monotone voice, kind of preparing myself for whatever news I was going to receive. On the receiving end, was a very chirpy woman informing me that although I had great answers and showed confidence, my experience was not sufficient enough for me to be Associate Producer. I think I swallowed my salvia a few times and slightly clenched my jaw together before I could drum up the nerve to say, "Well, thank you for the opportunity."

How can I gain experience if I don't get experience? This was the real question I wanted to ask her. I hesitated and refrained from uttering the question as to not come across as rude. Maybe I should have asked that question, but the reality was that the decision was already made. Before I hung up the phone, she said, "but we would like to offer you a Production Associate position starting at $7.25 hr." Upon hearing this; I had all sorts of emotions running through me. I was disappointed, upset, confused and downright insulted all at the same time. The thought of working for minimum wage with a bachelor's degree in hand was unfathomable to me. I didn't answer right away. I paused and told her I would get back to her with my decision.

Two days had passed, and after talking it over with my favorite counsel, my father, I decided I would call her back and unenthusiastically accept the job offer. I must admit, I was embarrassed to talk about how much I was making. I had this idea that coming out of college with a degree would immediately give me the world but the thought of me making less than what I was making at the bank gave me the angst. My father drew my attention to the opportunity and implored me to take the position because this was my foot in the door. He reminded me about the time he took a job at a fast food restaurant while working as a Welder. Someone saw something in him and asked him to apply for the job. The job paid less than what he was earning as a Welder. He didn't want to do it, but he did, and he later was promoted to manager. He was a Welder by day and a manager by night.

The first day on the job, I was nervous. I was given a tour of the building and was shown where I would be sitting. I had pictured this dungy, cramped office space with unattended coffee mugs, dusty old books and newspapers gathered everywhere. It was actually the opposite. The building was clean, neat, organized; everything was placed in order. It wasn't the 'Murphy Brown' sitcom scene I had imagined. Still discontent about the fact I was making minimum wage, and not getting the position I wanted, I unexcitingly smiled as I navigated throughout the building.

As human beings, we tend to have these high expectations, but when those expectations are not meant, we feel defeated. Have you ever felt like that? I was so self- conscious about making less than what I was making before getting the job, that I remember asking my father not to tell my mother how much I was making. You see, both parents had high expectations of me however my mother is the quintessential West Indian woman whose bold, exuberant, and at times critical attitude would dare not be challenged. Her opinions were strong and could almost come across as insulting. Her knowing how much I was earning would not have sat well with her, and my disheartened heart would not have been able to handle her reaction. She wanted to be content in knowing that her only daughter was earning a decent wage. Heck, I even led my friends to believe that I was making the big bucks now! Afterall, I was working among well-known, influential people. They expected that. I expected to land a top paying job as well, I expected to get the position I wanted. My 'expecting' all these things created a disappointment. I pledged however going forward; Instead of expecting, I was going to show up to work daily without having any expectations of anything or anyone but to simply go with the flow and do my best.

What I've learned is that expectations place too much pressure on the person that you're expecting something from, and the person demanding that expectation finds themselves anxiously waiting for that demand to be fulfilled, but then is brutally crushed when it is not. According to Steve Chandler, Author of 'Right Now', "The word expect creates anxiety and is fear-based. Instead of using the word expect, try making agreements. Agreement is so much more powerful." He says.

I expect you to be there for me. Instead say, "Let's agree to be there for each other." **I expect you to finish this book by Friday.** Instead, "Can we agree that by

Friday, the book will be finished?"

Agreements are typically made between two people or entities but for me, I had to make agreements with myself. It's less pressure. I agree to no longer have expectations. I agree to be who I am and accept who I am.

YOU SOUND WHITE

A huge part of being a Production Assistant is to book guests and conduct extensive phone interviews, all of which involves staying late at the office to complete the tasks. One evening, myself and other colleagues stayed behind until around 3am to finalize the following week's program. We knew it was going to be a long, relentless night but a productive one. We ordered sushi and pizza to feed our creative souls. I spent most of the evening booking travel details for various guests. I was speed dialing phone numbers non -stop to top notch celebrities in Los Angeles and had what some would call compelling conversations with some of their agents. What was not compelling however, was how presumptuous some of my colleagues were towards me in the way I was speaking. "Girl, you sound so white leaving those messages." A colleague said to me, who just happened to be Hispanic. She chuckled and stared at me waiting for my reaction. I looked at her quite puzzled but almost wanted to laugh at her. "What do you mean by that?" I was curious.

I needed some explanation even though it wasn't the first time I've been told that. I just needed her version as to what sounding 'White' really meant to her, so I asked her.

She lavishly threw her head back with a resounding laugh and said as she reached out to touch my arm, "Girl, you know what I mean. It's not that serious." I continued to push the subject at hand, wanting to understand what is it that makes someone sound this way. I needed to get her perspective.

She started out stridently trying to expand upon her bold claim by suggesting that it was the choice of words I was using and the tone of my voice while using those words. Words like: awesome, totally and absolutely. She also brought to my attention that my name was white and how I wanted to make the person on the phone believe that I was such. I didn't know how to respond to that implication because I thought I was speaking properly and in a professional English language where people would understand me. That is what we ought to do, especially speaking to professional people. I just remember feeling stunned, confused even more so since it was noticeable that my other colleagues co-signed with the notion of me 'sounding white'.

A quick snap out of my confusion, I leaned over towards her and touched her arm, then said with a smile, "Girl, you know how ignorant you sound right now?" The last hour into the night we all went into this debate about black sounding names, white sounding names, sounding white, sounding black. What does all this mean? My blackness is obviously 100 percent clear to me, but it was apparent I was being called out as to who I really am, not from my perspective, but from others. The concept of 'sounding white' carries a negative undertone and is a mere insult to white people in my opinion. I asked the colleague if she had mentioned to the producers who were white, if they knew that they sounded white. She once again stared at me as if I asked her a ridiculous question. I was really getting annoyed by her lack of knowledge about race. The truth is, you cannot sound like a race. Think about this, if you gathered all the Caucasian people from Ireland and gathered all the Caucasian people from Russia and have them speak. Do they sound white? How about if you gathered all the black African people from Nigeria and from South Africa, do they sound black? Do they sound white?

Making assumptions about the way someone speaks is not uncommon. The problem is when race is implied by it. Our conversation led to further discussion on which part of New York I was from. When I said I was from Brooklyn, a couple of the colleagues were surprised. I obviously didn't sound like I was from Brooklyn, according to them. When they couldn't fully dissect their definition of me, more questions were being asked. "So, you were born in Brooklyn, Bronx?" I then smiled knowing that whether I was born in Brooklyn or the Bronx- would not change their perception of me 'sounding white.' However, I had anticipated their reaction would be different once I told them where I was born.

"No, I was born in Jamaica."

"Jamaica, Jamaica? Or Jamaica, Queens?" The look on their faces when I told them I was born in Jamaica, the Caribbean, (that would be Jamaica, Jamaica for them) was a look of even more confusion to them, I didn't sound like I was from Jamaica either. So, the question becomes, "Who are you? And why don't you sound like you are from Jamaica? Why don't you sound like you are from Brooklyn?" These questions were valid, but to infer the idea that because I didn't sound like that, meant I didn't sound black? That was my issue, and that was wrong. I get it. Language is used to express pieces of who we are and where we come from. Race does not determine how we speak or how we should sound. Period.

I was reminded by my father, after I communicated with him what had occurred that night with my colleagues, that he too had to endure the "sounding white" perception as well. Because of that many of his peers thought he was better than they were or perhaps a little uppity, as if 'sounding white' is a better way to sound. It's just simply absurd. My father's British accent which he acquired broadly while living in England as a young man and well into his adulthood was often the subject of curiosity as to where he was from, primarily when he settled in the United States. He was perceived as unique. You see, although my father moved back to Jamaica after living in England, he still maintained his British accent. Also, not forgetting that my father grew up under the British colonial rule, his schooling in Jamaica was fashioned after the British system. All classes were taught in English usually by white British nuns or white Jamaican instructors.

Dad told me the story about the time he was booking his ticket to London over the phone through a travel agency and the travel agent on the receiving end asked him if he wanted any specialties while on the plane. She suggested that he wouldn't have to worry about not having his kosher meals as the aircraft served kosher delicacies. My dad said he wasn't anticipating that, but his quick-witted response was, "Oh, sure." He wasn't going to say no to additional perks that came with the trip. Of course not! She asked him if he wanted her to post the travel details in the mail, save him the trouble to pick them up, but he opted to pick them up in person instead.

When he arrived, he approached the desk and asked to speak with the lady who assisted him over the phone. He said the lady could not believe that he was Mr. Braham---- as the expression on her face looked like a deer in bright headlights. She looked up and down at him and she insisted for him to show his ID twice. She then asked him if he was certain that it was this travel agency, he booked the ticket with. He asked her to just look into the files and she would see his name. He assured her that she was the one he spoke to over the phone. Apparently, that agency catered to Jewish families traveling abroad to Israel and various European countries and it seemed as if that travel agent was not used to booking tickets for a black man before. After checking her files, she came upon a name, Alfredo Braham, and once again, an intense inspection of my father's ID confirmed everything. She proceeded to ask him if he was from London and where in London exactly, he was going? When she handed him the travel credentials, my dad said he asked her if the Kosher meal was still included in which she said, "Oh, yes. Sure." Oh, yeah, he did not want to miss out on a good meal!

My father might have spoken with a calm cadence but make no mistake about it, he was also unapologetically a Jamaican and proud. When he sat me down to discuss this notion of 'sounding white' he vehemently encouraged me to never allow others define who I am or how I should speak. He said, "You should speak so people can understand what you are saying, that's important first of all. But if you feel like speaking in your Jamaican patois twang, speak it to the right person who can understand that." He passionately reminded me that in Jamaica, our language and the way we speak derived from different languages like the Portuguese, English, and of course languages of Africa. I could not have imagined that evening in the office, speaking on the phone to agents in my Jamaican Patois because they would not have understood me. My father and I have experienced this bias as many immigrants have. We had to adapt to the environment in which we settled. At the same time, we are obligated to speak in any which way we choose without fear of being marginalized.

As we sat down to have dinner, our discussion led my father to bring my attention to one of my favorite Jamaican folklore poet and writer, Ms. Louise Bennett. He asked me if I remembered when I was a little girl in Jamaica in primary school singing Ring Ding Songs. I would recite some of her poems. I loved reciting her poems until this day. Louise Bennett was one of Jamaica's renown writers and performers. She denounced any form of condemnation to the Jamaican language and encouraged all Jamaicans not to be dismissive to the native vernacular, but to be proud. My father expressed those same sentiments. Dad turned to me around the table, knife and fork in hand, and proudly said in an almost indignant way, "Be proud and confident of who you are girl, and who you are is a proud black Jamaican, and also an American. Whomever don't like it, can go drown themselves." That was in true dad form. His words, not mine.

THE HAPPY WITHIN YOU CHALLENGE

Was there ever a time when you had misplaced expectations, whether towards someone or something? What or who was it and were your expectations met? If not, how was it resolved?

If you follow me on social media, I'd love to hear from you on this.

~ERIC LARKIN~

"A father needs to try and make provisions while communicating work in a positive way for his children."

Meet Eric Larkin, father of Shelbi. Eric was born in East Chicago in 1958. He describes his relationship with Shelbi as, "Great... she is a major part of my life." He was 34 when Shelbi was born and was quite prepared to take on the role as dad. Not a lot of fathers are prepared to take on the role of fatherhood due to various reasons, but Eric was. Here is my interview with Eric where I asked him questions about being a father to Shelbi.

How did you feel the day you became a father to a baby girl?

I was very excited knowing I was going to have a daughter. My job in the military had me away from home quite a bit, but I hoped I would be around more with Shelbi.

How prepared were you to be a father to her?

I was adequately prepared to provide for her, but I felt an urgency to be better (working, go to school, etc.). I was very prepared to profess my love for her and try to protect her. I still hadn't learned or didn't know some of the ways a man should prioritize his efforts.

What kind of a relationship you had with your own father?

My father and I didn't have a close relationship. It was somewhat adversarial. He was present, but very absent. To me he was larger than life, so unfortunately even his negative influences profoundly affected me.

Growing up, who were your father figures/role models?

Growing up there was really only my father. I pretty much looked up to men like Muhammed Ali and other men I admired that were in the public eye.

What kind of work were you doing when Shelbi was born?

I was in the military when Shelbi was born.

Could you discuss a little bit about the challenges you faced as a black man trying to raise a family in regard to examples about working, making ends meet, etc.?

My biggest challenge as a black man trying to raise a family was not having any positive, non-dysfunctional family settings as references. Becoming a parent at the age of nineteen, I was still trying to raise myself and having to undo what I was taught a man should be.

Could you share a poignant story about your everyday life experiences being a young dad? What affect, if any, do you think it had on your daughter?

There was this time when my supervisor (I was up for promotion at the time) spoke to me and addressed me as "Larkins." I tried correcting him, telling him my name is "Larkin" no (s). He basically told me it didn't matter. He can call me whatever. Perplexed, I thought of the promotion he controlled, but I also thought of my kids and what they would think if I didn't take a stand. My response was not pretty and unfortunately, I was not promoted. I try to relate the importance of character and to be true to yourself.

How different was it to raise your daughter Shelbi? What were some of the things you had to do or say to your daughter that you didn't say to your sons?

If walking through a wooded area, a crowd of people, or anywhere requiring navigation, I would probably walk in front of my sons to provide a path for them to follow. With Shelbi I would probably hold her hand. I also had a paddle (stick) called the "enforcer" that read "place butt here" and it occasionally found the boy's rear. Shelbi was given the choice of correction by talking and not doing whatever again and she never felt the enforcer.

What is the fondest memory you have of your daughter?

I have many fond memories of Shelbi and I together that I cannot pick just one. When Shelbi was 3 or 4 years old, I was working two jobs and going to graduate school. I'd be tired, but she would want my attention. I would say, "Let me rest for 20 minutes." She'd ask how she would know when it was time? I'd show her where the hands on the clock will be in twenty minutes. Shelbi would sit by the bed and in twenty minutes open my eyes with her fingers and say, "Daddy times up". Shelbi and I regularly went to a restaurant to have breakfast on mornings when I worked nights. I would write words on the chalkboard for her to learn while I prepared my room for class. The first day of school her kindergarten teacher brought her to me not knowing why she was crying. Apparently, her beret in her hair had come undone, and I had to fix it for her.

What are some of the goals you want from your daughter currently?

When Shelbi went off to college, I gave her a jar containing sand granules, pebbles, and rocks. I showed her you must put the larger things (important things) in first for it all to fit. I told her that it's the same in life; to always examine relationships and what she does because they affect her spiritually, physically, financially, and intellectually. I needed her now to be intentional about doing things that enhance or grow the parts of who she is.

Give an example of a time when you felt that your daughter let you down. What happened and how did you deal with that situation?

There have been very few times when I might have felt let down by Shelbi. One such occasion was her elementary school graduation when the graduates were shown on the screen along with short subscript. Whatever it was she wrote, I thought it was somewhat arrogant or superficial. At the time, I didn't deal with her about it. It helped me to realize she was her own person, and to see her not just what I would like her to be. At the same time, I also started trying to instill in her things I hoped would help with her decision-making process.

When you hear the words 'responsible fathering' what does that mean to you, and what can you say to new fathers or those who want to become fathers about it?

When I hear the words "responsible fathering" I think of ensuring your child knows they are loved, protected, and provided for. A father needs to try and have the things he does while also communicating work in a positive way for his children.

What advice do you have for young fathers today who might not be sure about being a father or who may not have the tools to support their children?

My advice to young fathers would be to embrace the absence of many of things they used to do because that void can be filled with some greater things, especially if being involved with your children becomes a priority.

What is the legacy you want to leave your daughter?

The legacy I'd like to leave to my daughter is you walk through life boldly and confidently. I want her to know trying is even greater than succeeding, and that I tried to accomplish things that required faith.

Can you think of a time you made a mistake with Shelbi? How did you handle that experience?

One time I was helping her learn how to drive. I was a little impatient, and I handled it by getting out of her way and letting her learn through Driver's Ed.

What do you see in your daughter that she may not see in herself?

I don't think she sees how smart she is. The skills she has used to navigate her life so far are the same skills she can apply to anything she wants to do. What have you learned about life that you wished you had learned at your daughters age? There is a season for everything, so be aware of them, and take advantage of that time because circumstances change. Appreciate and live within the journey, not fixate on the destination. See God in all you do and have faith. He will not let you down.

~SHELBI LARKIN~

"My dad treats me like a princess, and I love every bit of it. My future partner needs to know that I expect a lot, and I do not settle for anything."

Shelbi Larkin is a High School teacher who was born in Norfolk, Virginia. She is over the moon when it comes to the relationship with her father. During the interview with Shelbi I could feel the love and admiration she has for her father. It was reminiscent of the same "daddy's little girl" love I had for my father. She was completely transparent about her feelings towards her dad and gave amazing advice to daughters who might feel like their relationship with their fathers might not be the way they would like it to be. **How would you describe the relationship with your father today?**

Off the chain! My dad is like my best friend. I tell him absolutely everything! I don't know where I would be without him!

What is the best memory that you have of your father?

I have so many favorite times with him, but the best time would be when I was in kindergarten. My dad used to be a teacher at my elementary school. I looked forward to driving to school with him every morning and stopping at 7 Eleven to get me a donut. On the way to school he would teach me so many different life lessons. Before school started, he would take me out in the hallway with music blaring and dance with me. Even though other teachers would be in the hallway watching, it felt like it was just me and daddy and the world stopped! I will never forget dancing to 'My Girl' by the Temptations and 'O-o-h Child' by the Five Stairsteps.

How would you describe your dad growing up?

My dad was "Furious Styles" from Boys in the Hood, my Malcom X, the Leon from the 5 Heartbeats. He was funny, loving, kind, thoughtful, and always there for me. My dad is the smartest man that I have ever known. He always had the right advice to give. My dad never yelled at me, but just talked through situations.

Did your father ever speak to you about how you should choose a partner?

Ha, ha, ha! Now that I am older, he speaks about this every day. My dad is really big on my happiness. If a joker, as he would call him, is giving me any second thoughts then I need to drop him. My dad wants me to be with someone that is respectful, understanding, family/goal oriented, and compassionate. I tell my father about every guy that I meet, and I get his opinion to make sure he is a keeper. I will never date someone without my daddy's blessings.

Growing up did you feel like you could go to your father for advice rather than you would your mother?

My mom tends to be very dramatic, and my dad is more sensible, so I would go to him. I talk to my dad about all of my dating, school, and friend problems. One year, I was dating a guy in college and we were going through so much and I expressed it to him. The next day, he bought me plane tickets to go to Atlanta with him to be able to relax and get away from all my problems.

What were some expectations you had, as you researched how your father grew up? How has those expectations influenced your decision making in what you look for in a committed partner?

Man, listen. My partners have big shoes to fill. My dad is the busiest man I know, and he still calls me every day or calls me back in a timely manner. If my light bulb goes out, he drives to my house to fix it. If I'm in the hospital, he is right there. I don't open my own car doors or lift anything that's heavy. My dad treats me like a princess, and I love every bit of it. My future partner needs to know that I expect a lot and I do not settle for anything.

Give me an example of when your father disappointed you, realized it and later apologized about it. How did that disappointment make you feel?

My daddy has only disappointed me once in my life when he and my mom got a divorce. My dad was a hero in my eyes, so for him to hurt my mom was very disappointing. I think for almost a year I hated my dad. He constantly tried to apologize and make me feel better about the situation, but my heart was filled with resentment for a while. It wasn't until I was in high school, I realized I was happy they were divorced. I was able to see how they really weren't a good fit for each other and were better apart.

How would you describe the relationship with your father now?

UNBREAKABLE! THAT'S MY MAIN MAN!

What has been the most valuable life lessons that your father has taught you?

Character; no one is perfect, but character shines through everything. Nothing or no one should ever make me get out of character. When I let someone get me out of character, I let someone take control over me.

Do you feel your father has influenced you as to how to choose a partner or make decisions within a romantic relationship?

YUP! I would not date someone younger than me or in the military. He wasn't the best person in the world back in the day.

Give me an example of a time when your father was very supportive of you even when he knew you were not making the right decision.

Well, I normally don't do things my dad thinks are a bad idea. However, if I do something he does not like, he doesn't support me, nor does he look down on me. He just allows me to make my own decision. What are some of the qualities your father have that you would like to have in a partner? Tall, smart, funny, handsome, handy man, experienced, cultured, risk taker, easy going, good listener, determined, compassionate, respectful, and knows it is either my way or the highway!

What advice do you have for daughters who may feel like their relationship with their dad isn't the way they would like for it to be?

All dads don't have it together. Stop waiting for them to come around. You have to make your relationship what you want it to be. Don't ask, start telling. Show him the love that you expect to receive. Stop assuming and start communicating. Relationships are built over time!

What do you see in your father that he may not see in himself?

My dad is PERFECT! He always has to say a disclaimer about why he is the way he is, but I don't need that. I literally think my daddy does no wrong.

What was that one mistake dad made and you forgave him for it unconditionally?

He promised he would buy me a car at 16, and he did not! I was pissed, but I got over it eventually. He bought me one when I was in college, so it made up for it!

Explain why it's so important for a father to be involved in their children's life, particularly their daughter's life?

I think girls who do not have their father in their life search for love from different men all the time. Also, fathers help show their daughters how to carry themselves. My dad really monitored the clothing that I wore to the nail polish on my fingers. There are so many things I still don't do as an adult because of how my father raised me.

If you had one word to describe your father what word would that be?

KING!

~BINTOU BAH~

"A mother was once a little girl, and she can typically relate to their daughters. However, a

father has never experienced what it's like to be a little girl. Therefore, fathers being involved in

their daughter's lives becomes a special bond and a learning experience each day."

Meet Bintou Bah, a licensed Social Worker born in The Gambia. Gambia, whose nickname is 'The Smiling Coast,' was once a British colony known for its beautiful beaches. Bintou is the daughter of a very spiritual, supportive, and protective father. She says her father, M.A., prays a lot and he always calls his children on Fridays to pray with them for health and wealth. "Let there be no poverty in the home." Those words would be a constant message left on Bintou's voicemail from her father. Friday's are known as Jummah, a day where Muslims pray at noon. Her father, a devoted Muslim, instilled a strong spiritual connectiveness in all his children. He empathized the importance of education and dedicated his time to provide a solid foundation. "We all went to private school which was an instrumental part of our upbringing." Bintou says. In everything that she does, she and her husband include the expression 'Insha'Allah,' meaning, leave it in the hands of God.

How would you describe the relationship you have with your father now?

Our relationship is positive. He is a very supportive father. We have a good relationship, he calls me every Friday which is our sabbath, to pray with me and my family. Even though he lives in Gambia, he makes sure to buy a phone card and call me. Sometimes he doesn't get us, but he leaves the prayer on my voicemail. I've even saved some of those messages and play it back sometimes.

What is the best memory that you have of your father?

The best memory is having him witness my undergraduate graduation and cutting the graduation cake with both him and my mother.

How would you describe your father growing up?

My father was a strict type of father. My father had a lot of children, however me being the youngest, I think I lucked out a little bit with his strictness. Some of the conversations I would have with my father, my older siblings did not have. Being the youngest child, I feel our conversations were not so serious or as intense. He provided for us and made sure we all went to private school.

Did your father ever speak to you about how you should choose a partner?

No, that was never a topic of discussion. In my culture, that topic is a sensitive topic to be had because in my culture, our parents had that mentality that "a child has to know their place." We just don't talk about it. Culturally, back in those days, parents used to arrange marriages for their daughters. That was the norm. There was no discussion about sex, dating, nothing to that extent. As an adult, looking back, it sounds contradictory, because they want us to get married, but they don't want us to date. Times have changed, but I think that was one of the reasons as to why there was a shyness towards talking openly about that.

Growing up did you feel like you could go to your father for advice rather than you would your mother?

If so, talk about some of that advice. I would go to my father when it was related to education or business related. My mother, everything else.

What were some expectations you had, as you researched how your father grew up? How has those expectations influenced your decision making in what you look for in a committed partner?

An expectation I had was for my father to provide the financial needs for my education. I guess this is because he had already been doing it for my older siblings, therefore, I expected the same. I do also expect that a committed partner will contribute towards our children's educational needs.

Was there ever a time when your father disappointed you? How did that disappointment make you feel?

There have been a few times, and the disappointment made me feel nonexistent, but I have never mentioned it, because in my culture, it will then be deemed as a sign of disrespect to my parents.

How would you describe the relationship with your father now?

My relationship with my father is very good. We have a good relationship. I call him and check on him since he is living in Gambia. He calls me and speaks to his granddaughters. He has become softer over the years since all his children are now grown adults; his strict side has become softer. Our conversations are usually short, general and to the point.

What has been the most valuable life lessons that your father has taught you?

Self-Discipline. Because of this, I have learned how to be content with what I have and appreciate the little things in life. My Dad has always preached to me that in order to grow up, one has got to be able to make right decisions without needing an influence. I was able to stay by myself independently and sustain myself at the age of 19 because I had self-discipline, I learned from him. My father would always say, "Once you have self-discipline, you can live anywhere, you can stay anywhere and still be able to survive."

How has your father influenced you as to how you choose a partner or make decisions within a romantic relationship?

One thing I look for in a partner was the respect. I learned from observing my father and the way he showed respect to my mother. Romantic relationships were NEVER a topic of discussion in my household growing up, unless it was the announcement of someone getting married. My parents did not openly demonstrate affection either. However, I never saw my father argue with my mother. I never saw them fight with each other; not to say that this didn't happen, I just never witnessed any contention between them. My father is a prayerful man, a spiritual man, God-fearing man, so naturally, I looked for those same qualities in my future husband. Also, my father is well-known in my city in Gambia. He has kept a very strong reputation as being a highly spiritual, devoted, people-person. He is open and approachable, a peacemaker, and is engaged in multiple activities, especially religiously. These are qualities I would look for in a partner.

What advice do you have for daughters who may feel like their relationship with their dad isn't the way they would like it to be?

You make the initiative and guide how you want your relationship to be. This can make a big impact.

What do you see in your father that he may not see in himself?

He can sometimes come off in a hostile way, however, he is just being direct.

Explain why it's so important for a father to be involved in their children's life in particularly their daughter's life?

A mother was once a little girl, and she can typically relate to their daughters. However, a father has never experienced what it's like to be a little girl. Therefore, fathers being involved in their daughter's lives becomes a special bond and a learning experience each day.

If you had one word to describe your father what word would that be?

Pious. He is devoted in everything he does. He's known to be a man of dignity. He's a leader within his community, and a lot of people respect him and include him in their activities.

THE PROCESS OF LOSING DAD

He said
My absence is strong
And warm
It will hold you
It will teach you how to miss
How to be without
And How to survive anyway.

-Nayyriah Waheed

"Fishing. Take me to Modell's on PennsylvaniaAvenue so I can get some new hooks for the rod, would ya?" My father asked me in the sweetest tone. It was his favorite pastime, fishing. When he was a young boy, my dad would go fishing by the Rio Cobre then afterwards would dive right in for a swim. He would often boast to us children how he was a very strong swimmer, stronger that his siblings. As a young girl, I witnessed that to be true, as we had many trips to the beach, Hellshire Beach in particular. He even saved a drowning man once, who weighed probably three times his weight. Fishing, swimming, the beach, nature, those were dad's simple joys. It's not much of surprise that one of his very first poems he wrote was about his favorite pastime.

33rt3f4rt

PLEASURE SEEKERS

A float on silver deep, I watch the winding course

People sit with hooks and lines

Disturbing life beneath them lie

So calm, so cool, the water shines

A cooling splendor I enjoy A line vibrates, A handsome catch!

Contentment mingled with their pleasure

Dangling, struggling cries I hear

"Set me free I beg of you"

"Return me to my foreign deep" Cried a pained, distorted face

I seem to hear infants cry

On leveled land, on mountain peaks In the sky above me

and even in the depth below me

So, have a heart you pleasure seekers

Pack up your rods and bait

Go find your pleasure elsewhere And let those beneath be.

-Alfredo Braham

How could I say no to my dad? Of course, I would take him to get new fishing hooks! It was his morning ritual and he enjoyed every bit of it. His eyes would sparkle brightly while carefully cleaning the rods and placing the baits on the hooks as he would signal me over to learn how to tie a hook. I wasn't a fishing kind of girl and had no interest in learning how to tie a hook, but my father had a way of summoning me to learn something new, to get out of my comfort zone and pick up a new hobby even if I didn't care too much about it. "Just do it. Learn," he would say. I gave in, and I learned how. I also learned that spending quality time with him would mean more to me than he would ever know. Three months before my fishing hook lesson, I wasn't sure if I would have had that time with him.

SEPTEMBER 2013

A heavy fall unto the carpet jolted me to run to the downstairs bedroom. I heard a sound that sounded like shattered glass. I knew my father was in his bedroom, so I dashed into the room to see what the noise was all about. Whenever I hear sounds such as glass breaking, someone coughing, or better yet someone coughing while eating, my alertness thermometer goes up the roof. A simple snacking on popcorn creates an anxiousness inside of me, not wanting that kernel to go down the wrong pipe. The point I'm trying to convey here is, I am often paranoid when someone is or could be in the realm of any danger. Rest assured my alert radar goes up, and I will come to their rescue.

When I rushed into the room, I found my father curled up on the floor cringing his face. It appeared he had a bad fall and had hurt his left side. As I helped him up, he made a little bit of a grunt, signaling he was in pain. Apparently, dad was reaching for the glass of water on the nightstand and before he could get a hold of the glass, he felt a sharp pain on the side of his stomach. He reached out for the glass, lost his balance, and as a result, fell onto the floor.

I am my father's only daughter, so the need to come to his rescue was second nature for me. The feeling I felt running to the aide of my dad was all but pure love in wanting to protect him. My mother on occasions would always comment that If my father sneezed, I would immediately dash to his rescue. If he stumped his toe, I'd dramatically run to his care. I admit, I was always protective of my dad. That's what 'daddy's girls' do.

- **We Protect our fathers**

- **We Honor our fathers**

- **We Love our fathers**

It was an eve in the week, and Jeopardy was on the television. No one and I mean no one interfered with my father when Jeopardy came on. No one! It could be Mother Teresa walking through the doors or President Barack Obama, he would not budge. Perhaps Sarah Vaughn would have gotten his attention. Perhaps. He loved him some Sarah Vaughn. I asked my father if I could keep his company upstairs, so we could watch Jeopardy together. I helped him up from the floor with him still slightly grimacing his face, but he managed to walk out towards the living room bravely. Watching Jeopardy with my father was always a learning moment with short deliberations in between commercials of course. He would summon me to get a piece of paper and a pen, so I would jot down the answers and later research the topics. The highlight for me was being in complete awe each time he answered almost all the answers correctly. For him, his highlight was earning over 85,000 dollars one night---- not literally, to his disappointment, but he could have if he was on the actual show.

THE SHATTERED CUP!

A trip to the kitchen to make a cup of tea during one of the commercial breaks was a turning point for dad. While in the kitchen, reaching for his favorite tea cup, he made a very strong growling sound. I immediately ran into the kitchen along with my mother, only to see my father crouched over the counter top breathing heavily while bits of the shattered ceramic cup surrounding him. I remember franticly asking him, "Dad, what's wrong?" The cup was on the second shelving in the cupboard, and as he extended his arms to reach for it, a sharp pain at the side of his stomach pounded him terribly. He was in so much pain, he couldn't even lift his head up to say, "Get me to the hospital." Instead with his head resting on the counter, he murmured, "Get me to the hospital, this is not a normal pain."

Not bothering to call 911, I drove my dad to the hospital where I briskly proceeded to the front desk clerk in the ER. I was hysteric! "My father needs help NOW!" I screamed so loud that an elderly woman lying on a stretcher asked, "Are you going to deaf me?" I personally didn't care who I was deafening. I needed a doctor, STAT!

I knew that if it wasn't for my hysteria and quick action that evening, the nurses and doctors in that emergency room would not have scurried around my father so quickly. Even in his pain, my father stretched out his hands towards me whispering, "It's okay. Calm down. Don't worry." I couldn't calm down. When I see a loved one in pain, I want to shout out for help. I want to comfort them. I want to be there in any way possible. The doctors and nurses who surrounded him asked me what was wrong. My father placed his hand over the right side of his stomach then whimpered, "I'm in pain." He was then wheeled into the X-ray room. I was left at the registration desk nervously trying to hold the pen in my hand, not remembering how to fill out a form. I wanted to be by my father's side every moment, every second. After about thirty minutes, which seemed like eternity, he was wheeled out of the room. He seemed sedated. I thought to myself, "They must have given him some pain killers to numb the pain." His face was no longer grimaced, but relaxed and now waiting on the doctor for the results. I, on the other hand, couldn't bear to see him in that state. I had no choice but to drum up the courage, get it together, and try not to have my father see me get emotional, showing signs of major worries — especially not knowing the results of the test.

Finally, the results came in. Two doctors walked out to the emergency room. At this point my father was on a bed, sectioned off in a cubicle. For privacy, a draped hospital curtain served as a partition between dad's bed and the outside hallway. I was sitting on the side of the bed not wanting to occupy the lonely chair in the corner. I just wanted to be close to my father. My mother was standing up staring at my father then looking back at me, biting her lips in nervousness. I saw in her face, a look that said something was not right, the mood in the room had shifted, and it felt heavy.

That night was the longest I'd ever spent in a hospital. The scents coming from the emergency room made my stomach queasy even more. The saying, 'The crazies come out at night' now made sense to me. There were all kinds of noises and interesting characters. I witnessed one guy walking in from the street. He was naked, screaming, and asking for a soda. He then banged on the front desk. The guard immediately grabbed him while the nurse rushed over and gave him a hospital gown to cover him up. The commotion and the smell made me want to get out of there quick, but not so fast. The next words I heard were, "You need to have surgery tonight!" In that moment I knew our whole world would be turned upside down.

"We located a mass on the upper right side of the colon, the ascending colon." Hearing these words from the doctor, my mother expelled, "Rhassss." An explicit Jamaican word. My father looked straight faced at the doctor and said pungently with his arm raised in the air, "Take it out." His face showed he was determined to get out whatever was inside him. He did not hesitate to make that decision, especially since he was told that if he had chosen to wait another day, the outcome would not have been in our favor. Emergency surgery was scheduled for 11 o'clock that night. I watched my father's 5'11, 180 lb. frame wheeled in on a stretcher, telling us, "Don't worry, your old man is tuff." My mother kissed him on the forehead, "Love you Rue." Mom and I sat in the waiting room, just the two of us praying, crying, hoping and praying.

Surgery was a success, and over the course of the fall into the winter, my father had to get used to his new reality, a reality in which he tried to mask at times. My father was diagnosed with stage three colon cancer, a diagnosis he, along with all our family members wanted no part of. His stomach now housed a plastic colostomy bag, which protruded from his colon, as if it was an extra artificial limb. It was something he never looked at, he never wanted to learn how to change it when it needed to be changed. He wanted nothing to do with that colostomy bag, understandably so. This was life changing. He was a manly man. Walking around with a foreign object projecting from the side of his stomach was not manly.

In the weeks following my father's surgery, I pledged to take care of all his needs, to be there for him every step of the way. Doctor's appointments, trips to the treatment center for chemo, I did it all. Early morning fishing trips to the Canarsie Pier gave him an escape from his reality. It was his new norm.

The pleasure he received from fishing reverted him back to when he was a boy. He was giddy, he was calm, he was in his element.

THE CONVERSATION

My father and I had a lot of things in common. We were both moody at times and loved to crack a joke or two, most of them, dry humor. He would tell a joke with a straight face, almost as if he was having a go at you. He wasn't mad or angry. That was just his "joker face." His punch line was always on point and we both loved to write. The number one thing we had in common was the love for sweet treats. One morning I treated him to breakfast at our local IHOP, a breakfast and lunch restaurant that serves the best pancakes. Getting out of the car was different now for him. Not only was he self-conscious of the hideous thing hanging from his stomach, but he also had to make sure he didn't trouble the infusion pump attached to his upper right side of his shoulder.

"So, dad, how are you feeling now," I asked him. He looked me straight in the eye with a huge smile and said, "Overall? I'm feeling good." He started to rotate his shoulder in a shoulder dance. He saw that I was despondently gazing at him while smiling. "Don't you worry about me girl." He patted my hand. I told him I wasn't worried too much, but I didn't want to lose him. I wasn't ready. "Nobody is ever ready, but when it's time, then its time." he confidently said. Then he quoted one of his favorite poets, Robert Burns, "What is death, but parting breath?"

"It's parting of the breath, Allison. That's all it is. We still live on. When that day comes, I'll be going back to the soil and the world will still be turning and I'll be evolving in the spirit." Conversations about death are not easy, but my father made it seem like it was something beautiful. He wasn't afraid.

As much as I did not want to continue the conversation, dad gently touched my hand and said, "Death is a part of life, and although one can never be prepared for it, we have to accept it. If we cannot accept it, well, good luck." There's that dry humor.

Having that conversation was important because I was able to know how he felt about death, about dying. I observed his reaction towards the subject, and he was direct and honest.

His delivery about the subject was deliberate in tone. He didn't want me to fret nor did he want me to be sacred. He succeeded in that moment, but I was not ready. Perhaps deep down, I did not want to accept it.

- **How will you have that conversation with your parents? I strongly believe it's a conversation worth having.**

- **What kind of questions will you ask them?**

By the spring, I could see the changes in him, not weak or feeble but rather strong and determined to keep moving. He did not bow down to this hideous tarp! He would drive himself to Home Depot to buy his gardening supplies. He took pride in washing his car every Saturday. He prepared the soil in his garden for planting the most beautiful of flowers. There were red ones, yellow ones and white ones too. By the summer, the garden was the most colorful of gardens on the block. He was a gentle gardener, talking to the tomato patch, caressing the petals of the flowers with his soft touch, commanding it to grow and flourish, all the while, whistling at the birds so they would flock around the garden. He kept himself busy. He never complained. He was always on the move. I could see him getting his stride back and his levels were improving. By mid -summer, however, we were back at it. Doctor appointments had become a leisure activity. We were finding ourselves in the emergency room more times that I could count. There were moments where I didn't know whether I was coming or going. Routine hospital visits were not my favorite, but I bravely trotted towards those front glass doors, up those 15 steep steps, made that right turn towards those bright orange painted elevator doors. Ding Dong, doors opened, and I walked right in.

The elevator was my enclosed home for perhaps thirty seconds to a minute, where I was able to sequester myself in the far corner, taking in deep breaths as I prepared myself to brace any new -found news that might await me. I would walk towards the elevator and say, "Hello. We meet again!" before getting on. The elevator and I were friends. Once inside, my thoughts journeyed into a different realm. I would visualize that today would be the day I would get off the elevator, walk onto the floor unit, and waiting for me would be the doctors saying, "A miracle has happened, your father is going to be just fine."

I observed others in the elevator following protocol, looking up at the floor numbers, anticipating exiting. I, on the other hand, looked straight ahead, feeling anxious. The elevator dinged as the doors opened. For me, that sound meant it was talking to me. It was saying, "Time to face the music." It was my cue to exit, but I wanted to stay inside. I did not want to face the music. I answered back, "No!" I wasn't losing my mind; I was losing my father.

I went up on the floor and into the room where my dad was, but I did not see him. You can just imagine the panic I had. But, upon hearing he was moved to a different room, I was a little relieved. I entered his room; this time his bed was towards the back of the room facing the window. I walked in and noticed a gentleman who shared the room with him.

I smiled and waved at him. I then excitedly walked over to my father's side of the room and greeted him like I usually did, "Daddy-O!" in which he would reply, "Daughter-O or sometimes I would greet him by saying, "Father Abraham!" He would reply "had many sons." This was a reference to a biblical song about Abraham and him having many descendants as God told him. My father's first initial was A and of course when we put the last name together spells out Abraham. This gave us a chuckle and it was fitting as my dad had 4 sons and one girl. He did have many sons!

I eagerly walked over to kiss him and gave him the biggest hug ever. He then asked a question which was important for him to know the answer to. He smiled at me and asked quietly, "Did you say good evening to the gentleman?" He directed his hand to the other side of the room. I quickly said, "Yes, dad I did." His reply was, "Oh, okay. I didn't hear when you said good evening." The respect my father had for people amazed me. There he was propped up on a hospital bed, sick but still ensured I extended my manners to a complete stranger. That showed respect. No matter how grown I was, he was going to keep teaching me, reminding me of how one should show respect. You better believe after finishing up my visit with dad and said, 'See you later", I made sure I said goodnight to dad's roommate, this time, loud enough for dad to hear.

A telephone call from dad in the hospital alerted my mom and me. There was a different tone in his voice. Dad's voice had changed and sounded trembled. He asked us what time we were going to be at the hospital. He hadn't asked us that before. He needed to know because he needed us there as soon as we could. Once again, back to the hospital we went. During the car ride there, no one said a word to each other. My mother and I took turns as we sighed one after the other, there was no need to turn the radio on. We wanted to hear nothing but silence in the car. We approached the hospital. Right before I opened the doors, went up those 15 steep steps of stairs, made that right turn towards those bright orange painted elevator doors, I broke down. A sudden feeling of sadness came over me. My mother turned to me and said, "I know, Allison. Be strong. Let's be strong." She hugged me as the tears kept rolling.

"The doctors told me, there's nothing more they can do." Those words from my father's mouth brought me to silence once again. I sat beside him on the bed and said, "Well, that's what the doctors said, but miracles happen every day daddy." I was not going to accept this.

Perhaps I was luring myself in the abyss of denial, but someone had to have hope for my dad, and it was going to be me. He shifted his head unto my head with a chuckle and told me that I was his angel. "You always make me smile." he said. "This is the process." he told me. I selfishly became annoyed with the conversation we were having. A fury inside of me began to rise, and I was not going to yield to the notion that this was it for my father. I was going to seek out the best of the best doctors. I was going to write to the best cancer hospital. Yes! I was not going to accept this.

My discontented thoughts commingled with the nonreality of the circumstance. I was holding on to my father and did not want to let him go. My selfish ego was latching on every part of his being. I was waiting for that day to come so I could release myself from holding on, to release myself from the pain, and instead go through the process to be present in the now with him. I could no longer allow my obsession of ceasing the inevitable to bog me down. The day came when I wheeled my father out of the hospital one last time. I brought him home where he would be greeted by a hospital bed, which had arrived the day before. The reality could not have been clearer. Dad and I were going to ride this one out together, and I was going to be his earth angel.

DECEMBER 2014

If I was ever a reflection of my father, as most children are reflection of their parents, then I was going to exude strength and grace during this process. My father's fragile body was now becoming visible. His hair, now a silky, silver gray in color had a shine to it. I took great pride trimming his hair in which he would direct me to, "Go lower, close to the scalp. Real low." he would say. My brother Rue-Scott would shave his beard; that was his job. My dad loved it. His voice was strong. His grip was still tight. His mind was still there. His skin was still smooth. However, in the days ahead, unbeknownst to him, I would watch his face. It resembled a man deep in thought, lots of thoughts. I knew he was thinking, and thinking, just deeply thinking. I knew he was having conversations with himself in silence. But what were those damn thoughts he was having in his head? I wanted to know. Perhaps he was asking himself questions like:

Did I make my children proud?

Have I done enough as a father?

What kind of life will my children have after I'm gone?

I am not certain if those were the questions, he asked himself, but we sure did talk about how proud he was that he was able to see his children graduate college. He kept telling me how he knew for sure that I was going to be alright because he knew I could take care of myself. That was what mattered to him during his last days on earth.

Mozart, Eine Kleine Nachtmusik and Beethoven's 6th symphony filled the room, along with Sam Cooke, and Otis Redding. Dad would ask me to alternate the songs. Usually, during the day he wanted to hear Otis, or even a little Cocoa Tea, a Jamaican Reggae artist. The evening was spent with Mozart, Beethoven, Billie Holiday and Sarah Vaughan. It was a musical production as I would pretend to be the young Raven Wilkinson, tiptoeing while spinning around in the air, then posturing up my best arabesques, which I was clumsy at and could never balance myself. Dad would lay in the bed chuckling at the sight of me struggling to perfect my ballerina pose.

"What you think, dad? You think I'll make it to Broadway or maybe to one of Alvin Ailey's dance productions?" I was being silly but would do anything to make him smile. Dad stared barefaced at me and said in his dry, brutal humor,

"Girl, you're like me, you're not gonna make it."

He slowly shook his head and we both laughed so hard. Like Ali, he was my champion. Like Rambo, he was a fighter. Like the butterfly that floats high in the sky, cascading into the rainbow, my father's body transformed. His spirit buoyantly rose to a new dimension, covering me infinitively.

THE MAGIC DOOR OPENED

In September 2017 I took a trip to London, to celebrate my cousin's graduation from culinary school. It brought excitement, and I couldn't wait to celebrate with her. However, it was the end of my trip that would become a magical experience.

A visit to dad's old neck of the woods brought back nostalgia and warm feelings inside. My brother Mark and I gave one last 'Urah' for our father. We hopped on the train heading towards Aldgate East on the east end of London, walking the same path our dad walked decades ago when he was a young man living there with my two older brothers. Mark showed me the chocolate box, a convenient store where our father used to send him to buy candy and cigarettes. He even pointed out those same bathhouses' dad once spoke about. They were still there, only now, most of them were boarded up. He mentioned to me that a lot had changed in that part of town, but there were some things that remained the same.

We must have walked and walked for miles, and I was enjoying every minute of it. My brother showed me some of dad's cab routes he took when dad was a cab driver. My father once showed me some before when we visited on family vacations, but not as in-depth as Mark did. I could feel my father's presence as we walked by every crevice of the neighborhood, a neighborhood with a multi-cultured setting.

I was wearing a smile on my face the entire time. It was kind of an out of body experience as I daydreamed what life was like for dad back in the 50's, 60' and 70's. Glancing at my brother, made it even more blissful, as he was the identical image of our father.

Then the magic started happening! Dad's old apartment building where he and my two brothers once lived was now painted in pink and blue in color. A quick trip up the ramp leading towards the building, created more curiosity. We approached the front door, but it had a security code lock on it, so we were unable to enter. But Mark had different idea. We would wait a little while for someone to come out of the building, then walk right on in. It didn't take long before someone exited the building and Mark nonchalantly holding the door said, "Hello." We were in! With a friendly wave at the front desk receptionist, and with a steady pace, we walked to the elevators. We went up smirking. When we got off floor number 4, I couldn't believe how big and wide the hallways were with its mosaic tiled flooring. Each apartment had intricate designs on the front doors. "Hasn't changed much." Mark said. We continued to walk, and my tour guide brother reminisced on his younger self running up and down the hallways. Dad would be playing dominoes and Ludo with the neighbors. We approached the hallway where the door to apartment 43 was left open.

"That's the apartment! The door is open. Take a quick pic. Go, quick." Mark was surprised that dad's apartment was left open and quickly directed me to take pictures. We walked a little closer and I could see a glimpse of the kitchen inside. The door was slightly ajar, enough for me to see inside. I walked to the opposite direction where I could see the stairs leading up to the bedroom. This was amazing to see. My heart was filled with joy and excitement. We both looked at each other in disbelief. It was the only apartment on that side of the hallway that was open. Mark and I both looked at each other smiling. We didn't think it was a coincidence whatsoever. We secretly knew who left it open for us.

My curiosity became more intense, as I turned to look at Mark and said, "I'm going in, not without knocking of course."

"Yeah, do it. I'll step away." Not wanting any surprises, Mark turned around and walked away to the side of the door. A few gentle knocks would alert a very beautiful young woman, waltzing towards me. She had an olive tone complexion and appeared to be of Indian heritage, with her hair silky, long, black hair, her nose adorned with a gold ring. With a friendly smile on my face, I introduced myself and explained to her why I was there. I excitingly told her that both my brother and I could not believe that this apartment door was left opened. She then said to me that her mother just walked out to go across the hall at a nearby neighbors and must have left the door ajar. I asked with her permission if I could enter and look around a little bit. I would have respected her wishes if she had said no, but to my surprise, she opened her arms and said, "Please, come in."

My brother decided to stay behind and allowed me the pleasure of soaking in the beautiful space inside. He stood outside the doorway looking in and said, "It has not changed Allison. Everything is the same, just some fresh paint on the walls." I walked into the living room and stood there. First, eyes wide open, searching around the room, then I closed my eyes as I took in a deep breath. I had noticed while standing at the doorway that there was an outdoor balcony right off the living room. I asked if I could go unto the balcony. She gestured with a pleasant, "Yes, please. Go." This lovely lady had no idea, or perhaps she did, what this meant to me. The pink and blue concrete balcony was long and spacious, and it housed a few small potted plants. I stepped out unto the balcony and stood there, looking out unto a lush, massive, green field. It was a beautiful park. A park where my dad and my brothers would often frequent. I stepped closer to the railing, leaning over. Once again, I closed my eyes, took in a few deep breaths, slowly opened my eyes and looked out towards the trees, the view magnificent. A sudden calm came over me. I felt a sense of peace as I whispered to myself, "It is well with my soul."

~MARC JAJOUTE~

"Don't think negative. Don't talk negative; then you'll be a winner."

Marc Jajoute, father of Patricia, is filled with humor and lots of personality. He describes his relationship with his daughter as "Great!" Born in Haiti, Mr. Jajoute's upbringing taught him perseverance, discipline and a strong work ethic, which he prides himself in. Mr. Jajoute is a business owner and a teacher, showing no signs of slowing down at a tender age of 76. He's described by his daughter, Patricia as 'old fashioned'.

How did you feel the day you became a father to a baby girl?

I felt great because I knew I was going to raise a daughter to be successful.

How prepared were you to be a father to Patricia?

I worked hard, disciplined myself and respected everybody especially women. I knew that my daughter would grow into a woman. I hope everyone that she meets will treat her as I treat every other woman.

What kind of a relationship did you have with your own father?

My own father was my role model even up to now.

Everything he has taught me, I've applied it to my life, and it turned out to be a driving force for me.

Growing up, who were your father figures/role models?

Without a doubt my father!

What kind of work were you doing when Patricia was born?

I was working in New Jersey driving and loading trucks. At the same time going to school. After school, I couldn't wait to go home to play with my child.

Could you discuss a little bit about the challenges you faced as a black man trying to raise a family?

Ok, the challenged I faced, I always put myself to be a leader not to be a follower. Don't follow what people do for the well-being of the future of the children. I made ends meet by putting myself as a leader and graduating from college and opening a business.

Share a poignant story here that you can remember about your everyday life experiences being a young dad. What affect if any do you think it had on your daughter?

The story I can share is very excellent. I stand for my daughter to see me as a father. I don't go around playing fool with women and keep my head straight so when she looks at me, she understands the value of her father. I worked hard, disciplined myself, got up in the morning, went to school and did what I had to do for her to follow me as a father in every step of the way.

How different was it to raise your daughter? What were some of the things you had to do or say to your daughter that you didn't say to your sons?

It's almost the same. But when sons become 18, they choose their own way which makes it hard to change them back. One thing to remember is that girls are different from boys though. The reason why boys are different from girls, girls always look up to their fathers and boys always look up to their mothers. They have more attractions to follow their mother than their fathers. Smart boys will follow their father. But the smart girl, if their mother is smart, they will follow their mother. But the child that is smart will follow the smartest parent.

I would say everything the same way, but I would say stay in school, work hard, get yourself well educated and prepare for the future. But if you fall during the step, don't see that failure as a downturn, but use your failure as a step for success.

What is the fondest memory you have of your daughter?

My favorite memory of my daughter is that she works hard to deal with her bad days and works hard to change it to the best. She REVERSED THE CURSE! Everybody who tried to put bad things on her, she reversed it. And that is great!

What are some goals you want for your daughter now?

I would like for her to get her PHD. Also, to respect her husband and she respects him. I want her to be one hundred percent there for him, and do not look back or think back.

Convert all negatives to positives.

Give an example of a time when you felt that your daughter let you down. What happened and how did you deal with that situation?

My daughter has not let me down but there are some ways that can let me down. Like some negative thinking that makes me upset. Negative thinking and negative talking pull me down. Negative thinking showers you like hot water. I tell my daughter not to get upset when something happens because when you get upset, you lose control of yourself, and when you lose control of yourself, the other part going to be a winner, then you're going to be a loser. When you turn out to be a loser, people going to curse you. When people curse you, you going to be a product of their curse. Therefore, whatever negative thing comes up to you, REVERSE THE CURSE!

Don't curse, don't think negative, don't talk negative. Then you will be a WINNER!

What advice do you have for young fathers today who might not be sure about being a father or who may not have the tools about being there for not just their daughters but their children?

Well, the most advice I have for young fathers is to be yourself, work hard, get yourself well educated and don't let anybody take control of your family! You are the head of the family. Once you get married to a woman, your woman is half of yourself and a man is responsible for everything. The priority is taking care of your wife, and the children. Even when things do not work out, and your wife leaves you and take the children away, you still have to be there for your children because they are yours! No one will ever take better care of them than you do.

For fathers not sure if they should be fathers: Well, if he's not sure then he should not be a father. He may regret it in the future but now It doesn't matter what kind of advice I give him, because he will not take it into consideration until he becomes a father. Remember, nobody will appreciate what they don't have, only people who have appreciated what they have.

What's your legacy for your daughter?

I am a legend for my daughter because I always do positive things like work hard. I went to school, I opened my own business. Even in my old age, I am on top of my work, do things honestly and I respect people.

Was there a time when you felt you made a mistake with your daughter? How did you deal with that?

If I made a mistake, not only with my daughter, but with all my children, I acknowledge it. I understand it and I accept it.

Remember, anyone who makes a mistake, once he recognizes it and understands it, he or she can elevate themselves to greatness. But if you fail to recognize the mistake, you downsize yourself and people will not respect you.

What do you see in your daughter that she may not see in herself?

Well, my daughter always follows my instructions. What my daughter doesn't see is if she doesn't listen to me, she will be a loser (he laughs). Because the kind of experience I have she doesn't have.

What have you learned about life that you wished you had learned at your daughter's age?

Well, what I have learned is when a mistake happens, get up and fix it right away. When my daughter makes a mistake, she gets up and fixes it right away to better herself. That is what I've learned.

~PATRICIA WALKER~

"...the value of education and your independence!

These lessons led me to become a stronger woman and lead by example."

Patricia Walker was born in Brooklyn, New York to a Haitian father. She has always considered her father a wise man primarily because her father has always been consistent in her life. Their relationship is built on having strong communication. For Patricia, her father's old school way of parenting, she believes, is what helped ground her. A conversation with her father would have to be done in person, not over the phone. He values a personal connection with his children more than anything.

How would you describe the relationship with your father now?

Our relationship is stronger than ever. I am his 'parent' and biggest protector now! I have an excellent relationship with my father.

What is the best memory that you have of your father?

I have many favorites ranging from childhood to current day. From childhood, I would say when my father used to carry me on his shoulders. I felt so free and thought all other little kids were jealous of me since I was on the highest throne of course. Another one is when he taught me how to drive as a teenager as well as our father-daughter dance together when I got married.

How would you describe your dad growing up?

My father was very determined to maintain a relationship with me. My parents divorced when I was 18 months old, and when my mother won custody, she made it a bit challenging for my father to remain in my life. However, my father was very determined to maintain and establish a presence in my life even though it was only during school hours where I met with him in the principal's office.

Growing up did you feel like you could go to your father for advice rather than your mother?

Absolutely! I've always been a 'daddy's girl' and had a close connection with my father since he always paid close attention to me and was less judgmental than my mother.

What were some expectations you had, as you researched how your father grew up? How have those expectations influenced your decision making in what you look for in a committed partner?

I believe I've always expected my father to be there for me regardless of the situation, and my father always met those expectations! In terms of my husband, I expect the same. It's very important to me to have a reliable spouse who will stand by my side through thick and thin.

Give me an example of when your father disappointed you, realized it and later apologized about it. How did that disappointment make you feel?

Without going into much detail, one major disappointment was regarding the family business, which made me not want to talk to him for a while. My father noticed how hurt I was and arranged a meeting where we spoke, and I received an apology.

What has been the most valuable life lesson your father taught you?

He taught me the value of education and your independence. These lessons led me to become a stronger woman and lead by example.

Do you feel that your father has influenced you as to how you should choose a partner?

This question never crossed my mind prior to this. However, based on how my father treated me, it is important that I have a reliable, supportive and respectable spouse.

Give me an example of a time when your father was very supportive of you even when he knew you were not making the right decision.

When it comes to decision-making, I've always been on the conservative side, and my father ALWAYS supported my ideas and decisions. I can't recall a disagreement about my decisions.

Rather, he would give me advice on how I can fulfill it to the best of my ability.

What are some of the qualities your father have that you would like to have in a partner?

My father is a businessman and an entrepreneur who has a very funny and charismatic personality. This man lights up any space when he enters. Who wouldn't like that in a spouse?

What advice do you have for daughters who may feel like their relationship with their dad isn't the way they would like it to be?

It depends on the situation that led the daughter to have a fall out with their dad. My advice would for a relationship that is salvable would be to reach out and take baby steps. Depending on a person's background, some older folks thinks it is the "responsibility" for their children to reach out to them first. Sometimes our generation has to be "bigger and or more responsible" than our parent's generation and reach out to them, if that's what you really want.

Talk to each other. Most importantly, listen without accusations or judgements for a fresh new start. I believe once the relationship is not harmful or abusive, there's always time to start over before it's too late. It's only late once a person is in their grave, so do not have any regrets due to pride or ego. Leave those at the front door and focus on a positive do over. It's not going to be easy but continue to work at it.

Eventually, it may become what you have desired.

What do you see in your father that he may not see in himself?

I see in him the potential to do greater things if procrastination was not in his way.

Explain why it's so important for a father to be involved in their children's life, particularly their daughter's life?

It's important because no child should feel abandoned or deprived of a father or positive male role model in their lives. Just as it is important for mothers to be mothers, the same is true for fathers, so allow men to be men and father their children.

If you had one word to describe your father what word would that be?

I wish I had one word to describe my father. He's confident. My father is larger than life. His personality is big, and it makes others smile and laugh. He's literally my everything.

Any man can father a child, but it is a father's love and commitment to that child that helps define what it means to be a true father. The journey I had with my father gave me a better understanding of that. Father's aren't perfect, they will make mistakes along their fatherhood journey. As challenges may arise, whether it be how to financially provide, how to face societal projections and confinements, or simply not having all the tools to be the best father, the one thing a child will never forget, but appreciate greatly, is their father's time and dedication. This happy black daughter salutes you.

-Allison Braham

"A daughter should never have to grow up without a father or not knowing who her father is."
"Never be afraid of who you are, be afraid of who you are not"

Dear Reader,

Thank you. I hope you enjoyed reading The Happy Black Daughter. As a writer, the number one question I'm constantly asking myself is: What is my intention when I write? My intentions are to write valuable content that inspires. If this book resonated with you in anyway, or if there was one thing that stood out to you, please, connect with me. I would love to hear from you.

let's connect! Ally@allisonbraham.com

Twitter @allyblogger

The Making of a Happy Daughter and the 5 Principles You Should Take Away

What makes her a Happy black daughter?

The Happy Black Daughter is a daughter who is:

Surrounded by Love.

There is no greater feeling than love. Growing up I always felt loved by my parents, uncles, and cousins. When a young girl is in a safe, loving environment it helps to build her confidence. She does not feel scared or anxious.

Empowered by her Leaders.

Who are her leaders? Her leaders are the ones who encourage her daily, her parents, aunts, uncles, and cousins. The bond between a parent and child is undeniable, but so is the relationship with her extended family; her tribe. These individuals play a role in rearing and cultivating the sheer essence of a child, starting from infancy. The wisdom and strength provided by her tribe aide in her developmental growth.

Given Positive Reinforcement.

Growing up my parents would always hug and kiss me as way to show affection, especially when I would do or say something good. My mother was always hugging me. My father was the kisser. It is so important for parents to show positive reinforcement. This will allow the child to trust themselves and know that it's okay to make mistakes. Their behavior and the outcome of that behavior will be strengthened.

Capable of Expressing Her Emotions.

Every child should have the ability to express how he or she feels. A daughter needs to show her emotions without the fear of being ridiculed or shut down. A happy black daughter needs to communicate exactly what she needs because this will allow her to be open to help her. Express yourself!

Accepts her Self-Identity.

When the Happy Black Daughter accepts her true self and realizes that she is a product of her experiences, her parents' love, a product of her historical DNA, she is then grounded on the relationship she has with herself despite the behaviors and criticisms of others. The Happy Black Daughter is a daughter who is unwilling to give up her identity just because she wants to feel accepted by others.

When she is given these tools it's easy for her to parlay these five (5) success principles my father taught me:

Principle 1
Don't be Afraid to Sacrifice for Your Children

Principle 2
Get Up and Show Up

Principle 3
Always Be a Student of Life. Pick Up a
Book and Read

Principle 4

Hold Your Head High and Never be Intimidated by Anyone.

Principle 5

There's Strength Even in Times of Weakness.

THE HAPPY WITHIN YOU

Get a pen and paper or better yet a journal and start writing down the answers to these questions:

1. How has your relationship with you father made you Happy?

2. What are some of the principles your father has instilled in you?

3. Give three examples of how you are going to celebrate your father's love.

   a)

   b)

   c)

What are some of the questions you need to ask your father to get to know him better?

You are on stage giving an acceptance speech. You start by thanking your father then continue to elaborate more about him. What are some of things you are recognizing him for?

THE HAPPY WITHIN YOU
A FINAL NOTE

One of the greatest gifts you can give yourself is getting to know your parents. Don't be afraid to ask your parents about how they were brought up. Their stories are just as important to know as anyone you will ever learn about in history. The gift of knowing who your parents are, who they truly are is what will help shape your own life and give you a self of connectiveness. Spending quality time with your parents helps to create memories that will last a lifetime and you will evidently pass on that information to your children and they will do the same.

"What will happen if you just let go of your fears and dive into your dreams?"

"We need our fathers as much as they need us."